THE NARROW CAGE AND
OTHER MODERN FAIRY TALES

WEATHERHEAD BOOKS ON ASIA

WEATHERHEAD BOOKS ON ASIA

Weatherhead East Asian Institute, Columbia University
For a list of titles in the series, see page 253.

THE NARROW CAGE
AND OTHER
MODERN FAIRY TALES

VASILY EROSHENKO

Translated by Adam Kuplowsky
Foreword by Jack Zipes

Columbia University Press
New York

Columbia University Press wishes to express its appreciation
for assistance given by the Pushkin Fund in the publication
of this book.

This publication has been supported by the Richard W.
Weatherhead Publication Fund of the Weatherhead East Asian
Institute, Columbia University.

Columbia University Press
Publishers Since 1893
New York   Chichester, West Sussex
cup.columbia.edu

Cataloging-in-Publication Data is available from the Library
of Congress.

ISBN 9780231207683 (hardback)
ISBN 9780231207690 (trade paperback)
ISBN 9780231557085 (ebook)

LCCN: 2022025114

∞

Columbia University Press books are printed on permanent and
durable acid-free paper.
Printed in the United States of America

Cover design: Roberto de Vicq de Cumptich

I lit a fire in my heart—
No force on earth shall put it out
I lit a fire in my breast
That naught shall douse, not even Death

The one will burn while yet I live
The other for all eternity
The first I call the Love of Man
The second, the Love of Liberty!

—Vasily Eroshenko, "Humanity"

CONTENTS

CONTENTS

FOREWORD

THE PIERCING TRUTHS OF A BLIND STORYTELLER

JACK ZIPES

HOW CAN a blind storyteller see the world more clearly than most people who have their sight? Or, do we really have *our* sight? Are we born only to be blinded by commodified screens and rosy glasses? Do we need a blind storyteller to waken us to the conditions that tend to blind us? Are some so-called fairy tales too dark to bear?

These are some of the questions that came to my mind after reading Adam Kuplowsky's fascinating introduction to Vasily Eroshenko's life and unusual stories—stories intended to unseat us and tales that make Franz Kafka's stories, written about the same time, meek.

Like Kafka, however, Eroshenko embodied and lived his tales in metaphorical images that he could not even see. Many of them, as Kuplowsky points out, are sad if not pessimistic. Yet, in most of the animal stories, the endings reveal how life can be ironic and that we can learn from our mistakes. This is certainly true in "The Scholar's Head" and "By a Pond." In most of the Japanese tales, written by the grim Eroshenko, the major protagonists are talking animals or trees and plants that expose human frailties. They are portrayed in a dry style that enables readers to remain dispassionate and, at the same time, emotionally involved in the fate of these strange creatures. "The Death of the Canary" is a good example, for it deals with issues of freedom and monogamy in a humorous tone. But the tale about imprisonment and freedom that is the most poignant in this collection is "The Narrow Cage." Eroshenko not only raises the issue of animal rights but also condemns the pathetic ignorance and voyeurism of common people, who are not much freer than the caged tiger.

In all the Japanese tales, it is clear that Eroshenko had been influenced by the socialist and anarchist movements as well as by the Russian Revolution of 1917. His dedication to radical change often resulted in his being banned from different countries. Yet, he maintained an inimitable objective style in dealing with the brutality of humans who were no better than the animals they misunderstood and mistreated. Following traumatic experiences with the police in India, Japan, and China, Eroshenko changed his style of writing and became much more dogmatic, if not more pessimistic. Tales such as "The Tragedy of the Chick" and "The Red Flower" are desperate indictments of oppressive governments and the conditions that do not allow people to flower and use their talents to create fair and just communities. There is, according to Eroshenko, no remedy to a world that has denied freedom to everyone, from insects to eagles, from children to adults.

Despite the fact that Eroshenko's stories provide morals, they clearly are not your usual fairy tales, nor are his animal stories your usual fables. His narratives want us to see through words. They want us to open our eyes. They are desperate cries for help by a writer who wants us to understand what we are doing to ourselves, and how we are destroying the world, when we could be cultivating more just and joyous ways of living.

ACKNOWLEDGMENTS

MANY PEOPLE supported me during the planning, translation, and editing stages of the present collection.

Among the first to acknowledge its value were Ted Goossen and Meg Taylor, who kindly encouraged me to seek a publisher. A grant from the SUS Foundation of Canada proved indispensable in this regard, as it allowed me to take time off work to craft a proposal and enlarge my manuscript. Later, when it seemed that no publisher was willing take these tales seriously, Jack Zipes offered me a boost of confidence in the way of a personal endorsement. Finally, it was Christine Dunbar's enthusiasm and advocacy for this collection at Columbia University Press that ultimately led to its publication.

I would also like to express my great thanks to Diedre Goring, Yusuke Tanaka, Shibayama Junichi, Virlana Tkacz, and Julia Patlan for their invaluable advice when it came to translating difficult passages and gathering precious source material;

as well as to everyone involved in the copyediting of this book, including Kat Jorge, Ben Kolstad, and Maureen O'Driscoll.

I wouldn't have been able to complete my translations had it not been for some *very* patient readers, namely my brothers, Peter and Luke Kuplowsky, friends, Daniel Berube and Patrick Wang, and my life partner, Jessica Wei, all of whom were sources of endless encouragement and inspiration.

Last, great love and gratitude to my parents, Win and Walter Kuplowsky, as well as to the cats, Sammo and Rohmer.

INTRODUCTION

ADAM KUPLOWSKY

Give me a story about a disabled man or woman who learns to navigate the world and teaches the world, in turn, to navigate its own way around the disabled body. Give me power and also weakness, struggle but also reams of joy.

—Amanda Leduc, *Disfigured: On Fairy Tales, Disability, and Making Space*

A BLIND POET. An esperantist. A humanist. An egoist. A partisan. An anarchist. A "red" Russian. A "white" Russian. A Ukrainian. A child-like dreamer. A harborer of dangerous thoughts . . .

These are a few of the labels that have been variously applied to the fascinating yet largely forgotten personality that is Vasily Eroshenko. As a social activist and writer of political fairy tales, he sought to critique the oppressive institutions and conditions that incite violence and conflict around the world, and he urged people, young and old, to radically transform their societies. Despite the high level of fame—and infamy—he achieved in his adopted homes of Japan and China during the early twentieth century, he remains virtually unknown to enthusiasts of world literature. Because his tales are bound up with his fascinating life, and the fascinating lives of the people he interacted with, it is necessary to take a close look at his biography.

Vasily Yakovlevich Eroshenko was born in an affluent land-owner's family on January 12, 1890, in Obukhovka, a Ukrainian village in the Russian Empire. His father, a loyal subject of the tsar, ran a general store and maintained good relations with his fellow villagers as well as with the local gentry. The third child, Vasily was blinded at the age of four as a result of complications from measles. He described this traumatic event in his semi-autobiographical "Some Pages from My School Days" as having forced him to forsake "the realm of beautiful colors and brilliant sunlight."[1] From childhood on, he formed clear anarchistic convictions, claiming that his blindness had taught him "to doubt everything and everyone; to suspect the words of teachers as well as the slogans of authority."[2] At the same time, his blindness also taught him the value of cooperation and collective action. Throughout his life, he strove to fashion his deep-seated insecurities into a powerful motive for change.

At the age of nine, he was sent away to study at the Moscow School for the Blind, a prestigious imperial boarding school where he received a conservative education in the arts, sciences, religion, music, and basket-weaving. Although he later recounted that the school was "entirely cut-off from the world," an authoritarian prison where "students were at the mercy of their teachers," it was not impervious to outside influences.[3] During his school years, he immersed himself in the works of political writers like Leo Tolstoy, Maxim Gorky, Leonid Andreyev, and Mikhail Artsybashev, and became aware of aspects of Russian society that outraged his conscience. It was also during this time that he began to show a marked talent for memorization and telling long tales.[4]

After graduating, Eroshenko pursued a career in music and found work playing second violin for a blind orchestra in Moscow. Around 1911, he encountered the Esperantist Anna Sharapova, who introduced him to the international auxiliary language of Esperanto. Invented by Polish ophthalmologist L. L. Zamenhof in 1873, Esperanto was intended to relieve the "heavy burden of linguistic differences" that its creator saw as engendering social conflict on local, national, and international levels.[5] With its simple grammar and "international" vocabulary, it was promoted as a tool for nonhierarchical communication and was motivated by an "internal idea" of "brotherhood and justice among all peoples."[6] For Eroshenko, Esperanto allowed him to transcend the linguistic barriers that made navigating the world as a blind person a doubly intimidating experience. Furthermore, with its foundational texts of the Old Testament and the fairy tales of Hans Christian Andersen, it equipped Eroshenko with a moral and poetic vocabulary that was to resound in his political and artistic endeavors later in life. The profound effect that Esperanto would have on his identity, worldview, and art cannot be overstated. As he himself remarked to an audience in 1922, "keep always in your mind that my country is the world, humanity is my nation and my beloved tongue is Esperanto. Remember this thing and you will have the key to all my philosophy in all my writing and speeches."[7]

■ ■ ■

With encouragement from Sharapova, Eroshenko decided to further his musical education in London under the auspices of the Universal Esperanto Association (UEA). Aided by Esperantists across Europe, Eroshenko traveled by himself to London in 1912, where he was granted two months' board and tuition at the Royal Normal College for the Blind. Although financial difficulties compelled him to return to Moscow within the year, he left England with a solid command of English and lasting connections with the European Esperanto community. Moreover, he even managed an impromptu visit to Anarcho-Communist Pyotr Kropotkin, who was then living in exile in the suburb of Harrow. Recounting his journey for the Russian Esperanto journal, *La Ondo de Esperanto*, Eroshenko gleefully exclaimed that "Aladdin's lamp could not have helped me more than the little green star of Esperanto."[8]

Back in Moscow, Eroshenko drifted from his intention to work as a musician, and a feeling of wanderlust drove him to set down plans for his next journey. In London, he had heard about the respect accorded to the blind in Japan, and how they were encouraged to study as professionals in massage therapy and acupuncture. Intrigued by the economic freedom and social respect that such a life appeared to promise, he began taking Japanese lessons through the Japanese Consulate in Moscow. In 1914, again with support from the UEA, Eroshenko set out across Siberia to Japan, where he enrolled at the Tokyo School for the Blind, to study massage therapy and classical Japanese literature. Once settled in his new environment, he began expanding his network at Esperanto meet-ups and by teaching the language to his classmates.

Esperanto had seen nearly a decade of contention since its introduction to Japan one year after the Russo-Japanese War of 1904–1905. Hailed as one of the biggest fads of 1906 by the leading national newspaper *Asahi Shimbun*, it was embraced by seemingly unrelated groups, including anarchists, imperialists, missionaries, artists, and shopkeepers.[9] Perhaps because it claimed no affiliation with any one "culture" or "civilization," words strongly associated with European class- and race-based prejudices, the new "world language" quickly formed links with progressive politics in Asia, with socialists and anarchists as its most vocal supporters. Naturally, this association between Esperanto and radical thinking deeply disturbed the nation's elites, especially after the High Treason Incident of 1911, an alleged left-wing plot to assassinate Emperor Meiji. The ensuing clampdown of this incident was said to have ushered in a "winter period" for Japanese anarchism, socialism, and adjacent movements, including the Esperanto movement.

By the time Eroshenko arrived in 1914, the Esperanto movement was beginning to show clear signs of a revival. Although he did not come espousing any particular political ideology, he repoliticized the movement by virtue of his double status as a Russian and Esperantist. To those who had but a decade prior participated in the non-war movement—a massively popular antimilitarist campaign formed in response to the Russo-Japanese War—the nationally and linguistically unmoored Eroshenko seemed to embody the part-Tolstoyan, part-Japanese concept of the *heimin*, or transnational "common man."[10] In fact, one of Eroshenko's first speaking engagements in Japan was for the Heimin Kōenkai, a lecture series organized by anarchist Ōsugi Sakae, at which Eroshenko spoke in Esperanto about his meeting with Kropotkin in London. Unsurprisingly, the confluence of anarchism, Esperantism, and heiminism surrounding Eroshenko raised the suspicion of the Special Higher Police (SHP), which devoted its best resources to reporting on his activities.[11]

Over the next two years, Eroshenko formed important friendships with an array of progressive individuals who were working in different circles to solve pressing social problems and foster international solidarity on a nonstate level. Among these were the future president of the Japanese Blind Association Torii Tokujirō, American Bahá'í missionary Agnes Alexander, playwright Akita Ujaku, feminist journalist Kamichika Ichiko, educational reformer Katagami Noburu, and entrepreneurs and literary patrons Sōma Aizō and Sōma Kokkō. Perhaps the most significant friendship he had was with Akita, who shared his artistic beliefs and was inspired by his dedication to promoting pacifism through Esperanto. Immediately after their introduction in 1915, the two became constant companions at the theater, lectures, and literary gatherings, and collaborated on different projects. When the ruble collapsed in 1916, and Eroshenko could no longer receive assistance from his family, Akita was one of a handful of friends who helped mitigate his situation, setting him up with a lecture tour and encouraging him to write stories, which he then translated and submitted to literary magazines. Although Eroshenko's fame as a storyteller was still some years off, these early works, including "Easter," "Raining," and "The Tale of the Paper Lantern," each filled with romantic melancholy, won him his first public recognition as a "poet."

Hoping to establish a school for the blind in Southeast Asia, Eroshenko left Japan in July 1916, and spent the next three years traveling around Thailand, Myanmar, and India. During this transient period, he worked variously as a masseur and a teacher, published a polemic on the treatment of the blind in Europe, and collected folklore. When news of the Russian Revolution reached him in 1917, he decided to return to his homeland. Not only was he eager to participate in the ongoing political struggle, but he was becoming increasingly concerned for his family, with whom he had lost contact during the course of World War I. However, with British authorities eyeing all Russians within its colonial borders as potential subversives, securing safe passage to Russia proved not to be an easy task. Consequently, Eroshenko spent a hectic year evading the police, traveling between Myanmar and India, until he finally was arrested on the grounds of suspected Bolshevism in November 1918. When he requested deportation to Russia, the British apparently told him he would have to go back the way he came, and so he was put on a steamer bound for Japan.[12]

After Eroshenko returned to Tokyo in July 1919, he fell back into his former life among the Esperanto community, reunited with friends like Akita and Kamichika, and moved into the Sōmas' atelier at Nakamuraya Bakery. Eroshenko had briefly lodged at Nakamuraya in 1916, where he had formed a familial attachment to his literary patron Sōma Kokkō, whom he referred to as his "mamochka." Speaking to a crowd of Esperantists at a welcome-back event, he expressed his joy at being among friends who truly understood and loved him.[13]

Of course, much had changed over the past three years. Although World War I had brought unprecedented gains to Japanese industrialists, the overcranked economy was repeatedly shocked by recessions and depressions. Meanwhile, the socialist movement was developing with remarkable speed and unity, partly because of revolutionary victories in Russia. In 1918, female laborers in Toyama Prefecture staged protests against skyrocketing rice prices, stirring a nationwide revolt that effectively toppled the Terauchi administration. In 1919, Japanese progressives expressed solidarity with the anticolonial March 1 and May 4 movements in Korea and China. At the country's top universities, radical student groups like the Shinjinkai and the Gyōminkai were formed, and several political journals began publication, including *Warera*, *Kaizō*, and *Kaihō*. Topping off this political activity, the Japan Socialist League was established in 1920. If Eroshenko could not participate in the revolution in Russia, he could at least participate in the one taking place in Japan.

Through his Esperanto network, Eroshenko was introduced to highly political students like Takatsu Seidō and Ono Kenjirō, who encouraged him to attend lectures at Waseda University and to further his understanding of Marxist theory. Takatsu also invited him to attend Gyōminkai events and meetings at the Kosmo Club, a collective of Japanese, Chinese, Korean, and Russian activists working to undermine Japan's ongoing colonial efforts in East Asia. Gradually, Eroshenko began to add a socialist zeal to his humanitarian convictions, becoming active in revolutionary circles that did not always share the same objectives as those held by the more pragmatic circles with which he had formerly been associated. Consequently, as his friendships with people like Takatsu and Ono deepened, he fell out with older friends, particularly the Baháʼís. To be sure, Eroshenko was not an easy man to be around. When confronted with opinions that ran counter to his own, he could be stubborn, condescending, and chauvinistic. Even Sōma Kokkō referred to him in her autobiography as a "quarrelsome egoist."[14] Finding the right balance of cynicism, egoism, and cooperation would prove to be lifelong struggle.

Attending lectures and meetings left Eroshenko with few opportunities to earn a living. Besides, he was spending the allowance he received from Sōma Kokkō on feeding his activist friends. Noticing the toll that this lifestyle was having on his health, and recalling his talent for telling stories, Kamichika encouraged Eroshenko to write her a fairy tale that she could potentially sell to a magazine. The story that he brought to her was "The Sad Little Fish," which they published in *Shinkatei*, a women's interest magazine. Perhaps owing to the curious nature of this antireligious tale of ecological destruction, or the exotic air evoked by Eroshenko's name, the "The Sad Little Fish" proved to be a big success, and more stories were commissioned. Remarkably, in one year alone, Eroshenko published more than fifteen tales and a three-act play, placing his works in women's and children's magazines, national newspapers, political journals, and Japan's first proletarian literature journal, *Tanemaku hito*. Experimenting with the conventional tone and voice of the fairy-tale genre, he infused his quaint Andersen-esque narratives with unorthodox themes like police corruption, colonialism, social alienation, and intellectual dogmatism. And in brilliant twists of anarchist logic, he wrote from the perspective of plants, animals, and children to criticize the oppressive sociopolitical conditions created and maintained by adults.

When Eroshenko started writing political fairy tales in 1920, he was reflecting a certain trend in Japanese children's literature. Since the 1910s, conservative values in the children's book field were being challenged by a coterie of free-thinking writers centered around Ogawa Mimei, Suzuki Miekichi, and Kitahara Hakushū, who, through their journal, *Akai tori*, sought to nurture the innate virtues of children and to liberate the closed minds of adults. Their efforts were in direct opposition to the nation's elites, who for decades had promoted traditional folktales like the legend of Momotarō as a justification for an aggressive colonial policy, broadly recognizing the role of symbolic narratives in the socialization of young minds. Therefore, whereas children's literature was seen by the state as a tool for teaching *to* children, the editors at *Akai tori* recast it as tool for learning *from* them.[15] Certainly, this upending of the socializing discourse was informed by the concurrent development of strong social justice movements, rapid industrialization, economic unrest, educational reform, and the introduction of new ideas from abroad. In his fascinating book *Anarchist Modernity: Cooperatism and Japanese-Russian Intellectual Relations in Modern Japan*, Sho Konishi reveals the extent to which Japan's cultural revolution in children's book publishing was driven by an anarchist impulse to reverse the flow of power in various binary relations. It is no wonder, then, that many children's literature writers of this period—like Arishima Takeo, Akita Ujaku, Eguchi Kan, Ogawa Mimei, and Takehisa Yumeji—subscribed to radical leftist thinking.

Of course, no matter how strong the anarchist impulse was in driving this new wave of progressive children's literature, the high cost of beautifully illustrated journals like *Akai tori*, along with the basic ideological imperative of its writers—the preservation of childhood innocence in the face of brutal social conditions—tended to reinforce the value system of a middle-class readership.[16] In contrast, Eroshenko distinguished himself from his peers by pushing his anarchist impulse to its limit, questioning the value of innocence without social consciousness. This impulse can be seen in many of his tales, such as "By a Pond," "The Martyr," "The Death of a Canary," and "Two Little Deaths," where it is precisely the qualities praised by his contemporaries that lead his protagonists into dangerous traps set by capitalism, religion, and authoritarian systems. Although Eroshenko was indeed reflecting a politically driven trend in children's literature, he also was expanding it, anticipating the arrival of a Japanese proletarian children's literature in the late 1920s and 1930s.[17]

In addition to being a producer of fairy tales, Eroshenko became a sort of fairy-tale production himself. The fact that he always dressed in a Ukrainian peasant blouse and carried a balalaika, with which he sang romantic ballads and rousing political songs, aligned well with the popular image of him as a transnational common man.[18] And like a fairy-tale hero, he was often described by his supporters with infantilizing literary signifiers, such as "ruddy cheeks," a "soft feminine face," and a "pure heart."[19] Furthermore, his wanderings were interpreted in quest-like terms, and his blindness as a powerful moral force, as evidenced by the following piece by liberal critic Hasegawa Nyozekan: "His sightless eyes cannot make him unhappy. The world he saw for but a short time with the heart of a small child was all that he has seen with his own eyes. Nevertheless, this made him happy. His eyes could not develop the distinction of skin color, the reason that man has tormented man. His eyes also cannot see the horrible colors that divide the world map and incite war. Now his eyes see the skin of man and the world map in monochrome, and he roams across a singular world."[20]

When Nakamura Tsune and Tsuruta Goro unveiled their paintings of Eroshenko in 1921 to domestic and international acclaim, the image of "the blind poet" and "partisan" from an idealized version of Russia was cemented in the public's mind.[21] Even after his years in Japan, Eroshenko continued to appear as a character in poems, plays, and short stories by well-known Japanese authors like Akutagawa Ryūnosuke, Kusano Shimpei, Tsuji Jun, and Ehara Koyata.[22]

But Eroshenko's life was hardly a fairy tale. Since his return to Japan in 1919, the SHP had regarded his surging popularity, particularly as a public speaker, as a threat to social order, collaborating with the British Foreign Office to report on his many activities and connections. One of their concerns lay in the sheer emotional support he seemed to elicit from the public. A Gyōminkai event on April 16, 1921, at which Eroshenko delivered an impassioned speech entitled "The Cup of Misfortune" drew in well over a thousand people despite heavy police presence. Action was finally taken when, after two arrests in 1921—first at a May Day march, and a week later at a Japan Socialist League convention—Eroshenko was arrested for a third time and was deported from Japan for harboring "dangerous thoughts."[23] Writing for the *Yomiuri Daily*, Eguchi Kan described the horrific details of this third and final arrest, which took place in the middle of the night at Nakamuraya:

> After trampling on the terrified man [Eroshenko], they [the police] grabbed him by his hands and feet and hauled him downstairs, where they shoved him repeatedly to the ground. Then, turning a deaf ear to his cries for help, they dragged him over the gravel streets of Shinjuku to Yodobashi Police Station. . . .
>
> [At the station], the incredulous Japanese authorities are said to have continuously asked him if he really was blind. Unable to satisfy their fathomless doubt, they went so far as to forcibly pull back his eyelids. I wonder what they thought of their contemptible suspicions when at last they discovered he really was blind?[24]

When the public learned of Eroshenko's arrest and the fuzzy grounds for his deportation, there was a tremendous uproar. Newspaper articles and letters to the editor were written; a young girl wrote a poem expressing her sympathy for the poet; and funds were raised for his travel expenses. To the everyday observer, Eroshenko was simply a fairy-tale writer, if not a fairy-tale hero, who wore a humble rubashka, sang folk songs, and spoke on the need for transnational cooperation. According to a detailed police report on public opinion, his biggest sympathizers at the time of his arrest and deportation were women, socialists, and artists.[25]

The Japanese public were not alone in expressing its contempt at the gross mistreatment of Eroshenko. Following the story from China, a soon-to-be-famous Lu Xun—he had not yet published his first collection of stories—felt compelled to translate the author's most recent tale, "A Narrow Cage," for *New Youth*, the flagship journal of the anti-imperialist, antitraditionalist New Culture movement centered around scholars and writers at Beijing University. His aim, as he saw it, was to "transmit the pained cry of one who had been abused" and so "elicit rage and disgust against those in power."[26] Chinese intellectuals readily embraced Eroshenko's tale of a tiger driven mad by the psychological prison of colonial oppression, reading into it the trauma they themselves had been dealt by foreign aggressors since the later decades of the nineteenth century. On a more creative level, Lu Xun was clearly drawn to Eroshenko's poetic style and narrative techniques. In fact, Andrew F. Jones has argued that Eroshenko's works bore an uncanny resemblance to Lu Xun's own, particularly in their "recursive and ultimately unsustainable narrative structure, in which awakening is merely a dream, and the dream an awakening to disenchantment or death."[27]

On June 4, 1921, Eroshenko was deported from Japan; and two days later, he arrived in Vladivostok, then under the control of anti-Bolshevik forces. From there, he endeavored to travel by train and foot into Red Russia, making it as far as Iman, where the Chita government refused to allow him to cross the border on account of his not being a communist. After waiting for three weeks in a pest-ridden freight train while the Chita authorities looked into his personal file, Eroshenko headed south to Harbin, China. In Harbin, he lodged with Japanese expatriates, wrote three accounts of his recent trials, and began reaching out to the local Esperanto community for help. One person who responded to Eroshenko's call was Hu Yuzhi, a UAE member in Shanghai. Hu invited Eroshenko to Shanghai, where he secured him a teaching position at the Shanghai Esperanto School. Thanks to Lu Xun's efforts, coverage of Eroshenko's arrival in the *Chenbao Fukan*, a literary supplement to the *Beijing Chenbao*, portrayed him as an international celebrity whose status was on par with that of Bertrand Russel, Rabindranath Tagore, and George Bernard Shaw, all of whom visited China during this period.[28]

While in Shanghai, Eroshenko organized fundraising concerts for the Shanghai Esperanto School and began working on his first piece of Esperanto fiction, "The Tales of a Withered Leaf." A cycle of dark prose-poems, "Tales" was an outpouring of grief for the Chinese people, whom Eroshenko viewed as victims of political corruption, cultural conservatism, and foreign imperialism. Although excessive in its attack on traditional Chinese values and practices, his commentary was entirely in line with the currents of the New Culture movement, which, in the words of *New Youth* editor-in-chief Chen Duxiu, had been warning "of the incompatibility between Confucianism and the new belief, the new society, and the new state" of China since 1916.[29] Grieving the shipwreck of his "ferry of happiness" and looking to insert himself into this movement, in 1922, Eroshenko accepted an offer from Cai Yuanpei, the dean of Beijing University, to teach Esperanto and Russian literature at the university. Knowing that Eroshenko did not speak Chinese,

Cai reached out to Lu Xun and his brother Zhou Zuoren, both of whom could speak fluent Japanese. The Zhou brothers were more than happy to have Eroshenko stay with them at their home in Beijing.

Since its inception, the New Culture movement had made a project of establishing a vernacular literature that would raise the consciousness of the masses. Responding to various developmental and socializing discourses circulating the globe, New Culture critics like Lu Xun, Zhou Zuoren, Zhao Jingshen, Chen Bochui, and Hu Yuzhi turned to children's literature as an incubator for such a project.[30] Specifically, they held up Eroshenko's fairy tales as the model for a new type of children's literature and as a tool for developing the nation through its youth. "After Andersen came Wilde, and after Wilde came Eroshenko," remarked Zhao in the *Chenbao Fukan*: "so that through the eyes of literature, art is gradually progressing! . . . Perhaps we should use just such a progression—from Andersen to Wilde to Eroshenko—to lead children forward as they gradually mature from infancy to adolescence."[31]

■ ■ ■

In February 1922, Eroshenko arrived in Beijing to much fanfare.[32] The capital was the center not only of the New Culture movement but also of China's anarchist and communist movements. As in Japan, each political group saw in Eroshenko the embodiment of their imagined Russia. Consequently, his lectures at Beijing University, where he was promised a generous salary of $200 a month, initially were well attended.

At the Zhou residence, he was provided with a secretary and treated like family. When not teaching, he entertained Japanese, Chinese, and Korean anarchists, or he turned his hosts' courtyard into a vegetable garden and petting zoo, with chicks, ducklings, and tadpoles. Given these ideal circumstances, one would expect that Eroshenko was very happy in Beijing. This, however, was not the case. "This place is so lonely," he famously complained to Lu Xun, "As lonely as the desert!"[33] In Zhou Zuoren's opinion, Eroshenko suffered from a double longing for Japan and Russia, observing that he "yearned for Japan like a lover; but having lost at love, was redirecting his affection solely at his mother [Russia]."[34] Indeed, like the spring breeze in his tale "The Isle of Dreams," Eroshenko's thoughts were flying off to "the faraway North, to the land of the Snow and the world-turning Spirit."[35]

Longing to hear the nightingales of his dear Ukraine, and eager to reunite with his family, Eroshenko left Beijing for Europe in the summer of 1922. Although he had left most of his belongings behind, the Zhou brothers did not expect their wayfaring friend to return anytime soon, and each published a literary reminiscence to commemorate his stay. Lu Xun's piece, "The Comedy of the Ducks," a parody of Eroshenko's tale "The Tragedy of the Chick," was a particularly heartfelt send-up of his foreign guest's overambitious nature that is widely read by Chinese schoolchildren to this day.[36]

After attending the Fourteenth Universal Esperanto Congress in Finland, Eroshenko returned to Russia for the first time in eight years. In Moscow, he met up with Wada Kiichirō, an anarchist from Japan, and together the two traveled to

Obukhovka. Wada recorded an account of their turbulent journey in a travelogue entitled "With Eroshenko in Ukraine."

Despite his suspicions about the Communist Party, whose policies he criticized as the worst of any state, Eroshenko had always envisioned revolutionary Russia, if not in practice, then at least in spirit, as a transformative "land of rainbows." His vision, however, could not have been further from the truth. Like the anarchist Emma Goldman, who had left Russia a year earlier, he had hoped to find in Russia a newborn country wholly dedicated to the revolutionary cause. Instead, he found that the Bolsheviks had imposed a brutal surveillance state and had done little to raise the consciousness of the masses.[37] To make matters worse, his family had fallen on hard times: their land had been taken away and their house had been burned down. Not long after his visit home, Eroshenko channeled his bitter experience into a new tale entitled "Father Time." A parable on the cyclically destructive tendency of mankind, it reflects his growing awareness that revolution without the fundamental change of social and economic relations would always lead to autocracy, if not tyranny.

When Eroshenko returned to Beijing in November, his former celebrity status had all but faded. While there had been initial enthusiasm for his university lectures, his students were left unimpressed, and enrollment dwindled. This low enrollment was due to several reasons—the first being that Eroshenko did not speak Chinese, a fact that, despite the efforts of his interpreters, must have put a wall between him and his students. Second, his criticisms of Bolshevism offended the pro-Bolshevik camp at the university. Third, and most important, he held a negative opinion of the Chinese intellectual class, criticizing students, teachers, writers, socialists, and anarchists in China for lacking what he saw as a spirit of self-sacrifice. As Xiaoqun Xu has keenly observed, "while criticizing capitalism and Western governments' policies, he cherished Russian literature, theater, music, and visual arts, and scolded educated Chinese for lacking tastes in all these. . . . [Thus] coming from a different locus (and personal experience) in the colonial world order, [Eroshenko] would reach a position of dismissing Chinese culture and reinforcing the cultural power of the West."[38]

It might be said that Eroshenko was merely repackaging sentiments expressed by Lu Xun—and one need only read the latter's stories "A Village Opera" and "Dragon Boat Festival" to sense this—but to reiterate Xu's analysis, Eroshenko was indeed speaking from a different locus; and the alleged notion that he was unable to distinguish race did not change the fact that he was a white man criticizing Asian people for being "culturally backward."

The final straw came in December, after Eroshenko wrote a scathing review of a play put on by the Beijing University Experimental Theater Group. In it, he denounced the group for perpetuating what he saw as the "barbaric custom" that prevented women from performing on stage with men. He bemoaned the fact that there was "no good theater in China," comparing the male students playing females to "monkeys imitating human beings."[39] Needless to say, his criticisms were an affront to the young performers, and a war of words broke out in the *Chenbao Fukan*—one that sadly turned into an attack on Eroshenko's blindness. Although the Zhou brothers came to Eroshenko's defense, and Eroshenko offered a half apology for his review, it was too late—the damage was done. In January 1923, sensing poor enrollment, he canceled the rest of his lectures at Beijing University. In that same month, when he began to get harassed by the Japanese foreign press and the Chinese authorities about his connection to Ōsugi Sakae, he decided that it was time for him to return to Russia.

If he found some hope and contentment before leaving China, it came in the form of an unexpected visitor. The visitor was Gōzō Yoneda, a sixteen-year-old high-school dropout from Hiroshima, who had worked his way to Beijing in the hope of meeting his literary idol. Eroshenko befriended the young man and agreed to pay for his fare back to Japan in exchange for secretarial work. The result of this exchange was "The Red Flower," the last fairy tale that Eroshenko was to publish in his lifetime. A literary mash-up of first-person narrative and third-person allegory, it told the story of a depressed artist and his idealistic young student experiencing a series of visions that culminate in the man passing on to the student the dying flame of his revolutionary spirit. As in the tale, Eroshenko can be said to have passed on his revolutionary spirit to Yoneda, who would later change his name to "Karl" Yoneda, and become a well-known labor organizer in the United States.

On April 16, Eroshenko packed his bags and left China for good. Despite the damage that had been done to his reputation among students at Beijing University, the Zhous were loath to see him go, and he continued to be remembered favorably by writers like Ye Shengtao, He Qifang, Xiao Hong, and Xie Bingying. In the foreword to a 1930 collection of Eroshenko's fairy tales translated into Chinese, anarchist and novelist Ba Jin expressed: "Eroshenko is our familiar and esteemed friend . . . [He] took the sorrow of mankind as his own, loving mankind more than he loves himself. Like a musician, he put his love of man and his hatred of our social system into a chord played with a beautiful and sad style that has touched our hearts."[40] More than a decade after his departure, literary critic Lin Yutang still considered Eroshenko to be relevant to Chinese readers, ranking him alongside Andreyev and Artsybashev as one of the most popular Russian writers in the country.[41] Even to this day, several of his tales are widely accessible by way of Lu Xun's ever-popular collected works.

For the next year, Eroshenko traveled around Europe, attending Esperanto congresses and trying to build a network of blind Esperantists. After returning to Moscow in the fall of 1924, he was invited to work as a Japanese interpreter at the Communist University of the Toilers of the East (KUTV), where he worked with Katayama Sen, one of the founders of the American and Japanese Communist Parties. Kazama Jōkichi, a student at the university, was surprised to see that Eroshenko had not flourished in Soviet Russia, recalling that "[h]e was dressed in ragged clothes and living in a basement. . . . While the Japanese police had labeled him a 'Red,' here in the Red City he was seen as a 'White' or a 'Gray.'"[42] Eroshenko's criticism of the Communist Party eventually drew the ire of Katayama and the student body, and, perhaps for ideological reasons, he decided to leave the university in 1928. One can only imagine the hard feelings that this inspired, as he had long hoped to play an important role in Russia's reconstruction.

From 1928 to 1929, Eroshenko lived on the Chukchi Peninsula, in northernmost Siberia, where his brother Alexander was working as a veterinarian. During his stay, he collected folklore and studied the situation of the local blind population, possibly for the All-Russia Association of the Blind, with which he was associated at the time. In the early 1930s, he began writing sketches, poetry, and essays inspired by his experiences among the Chukchi people, many of which were published in the braille periodical *Esperanto Ligilo*. These writings are said to be among Eroshenko's finest contributions to Esperanto literature, and, moreover, they offer a strong rebuke of Soviet bureaucracy and European civilization, which he viewed as self-destructive and "fatally stupid."[43] They are even more remarkable when one considers that they were written around the time of Stalin's Great Purge.

Throughout the 1930s, Stalin and the People's Commissariat for Internal Affairs initiated a series of show trials and covert executions to remove rival influences in the Communist Party. Amidst this culture of deadly paranoia, Soviet Esperantists were but one group that was singled out as a threat to party stability, particularly for their transnational networks, which were feared to be full of spies. Charged as "Trotskyite counter-revolutionaries" and "socially dangerous elements," many Esperantists were sent to labor camps or summarily executed for little reason beyond possessing Esperanto literature or international correspondence.[44] This dire situation may explain why, in 1934, Eroshenko fled to Kushka, in Turkmenistan, where he worked for several years as a teacher at a school for blind children. Writing to a friend in 1940, he expressed the concern he had for his own safety as well as that of his Esperanto-speaking peers: "You must write to me in Russian. Esperanto is no longer in fashion. All of the central Esperanto institutions are closed, and many Esperantists have been arrested as spies and traitors. For this reason, I have stopped writing to my foreign friends. Only rarely do I receive copies of *Esperanto Ligilo*. Are you receiving anything from abroad?"[45] This period in Eroshenko's life was not all bleak, however. The students at his school were fond of their globe-trotting teacher, who encouraged independent thinking, organized literary workshops, staged plays, and shared tales about people from all over the world.[46] In 1936, Eroshenko pioneered a variant of braille that corresponded with the Turkmen alphabet; and, in 1938, he made a trip to Leningrad, where he came in third place in an all-Russian chess tournament for the blind.

The outbreak of World War II in 1939 must have been disheartening to the humanist Eroshenko, but it hardly could have come as a surprise. In fact, he had foreseen its eventuality since the end of the last war, at which time he criticized international relations as an outright scam, in which groups of countries ganged up on other countries to stir up conflict and profit off the terrible results.[47] Besides predicting a war between Japan and the United States, he had ominously warned about the dangers of ethno-nationalism, arguing that ethnic biases were laid and maintained by "politicians, patriots and scientists . . . and should they become the core principles of a national education system or religious dogma, it will be near impossible to imagine to what absurd ends they will lead man."[48] How exactly Eroshenko rode out the war remains a mystery, as by this time he was publishing infrequently and his correspondence was being intercepted by government agents.

After the end of World War II, Eroshenko briefly resumed his former life in Moscow, teaching at his alma mater, the Moscow School for the Blind. Then, in 1949, he returned to his native village to recover from a "tortuous and lasting" illness, which turned out to be cancer. On December 23, 1952, he died and was buried in his village cemetery, unrecognized as a storyteller in both Russia and Ukraine. Not even his friends in Japan or China were to learn the news of his passing until years later, when the Russian translator Vladimir Rogov noted his name in Lu Xun's "The Comedy of the Ducks" and began looking into his life. According to family and friends, Eroshenko continued to write until his final days. Fortunately, some of his last works were preserved, but most of his personal archive is said to have been confiscated by the secret police and likely disposed of.

■ ■ ■

Today, when I read news of the ecological destruction of stolen indigenous lands by bankers and bureaucrats across the Americas; the removal of homeless encampments by militarized police forces in Toronto, Paris, and Tokyo; the brutal working conditions on the warehouse floors of mega-corporations like Amazon; and the rising tensions between capitalist empires like Russia, the United States, and China, I cannot help but recall Eroshenko's 1921 speech, "A Cup of Misfortune," in which he fiercely contests the conservative view that the world's existential crisis is nothing more than the exaggerated fear of overly sensitive progressives: "It is said that a house will catch fire after the mice have left it. But in reality, the mice only leave because the house is already on fire. Likewise, it is said that a river will flood after the ants have left it. But in reality, the ants only leave because the river is already flooded. Well then, conservatives say that the world will descend into chaos after the socialists and workers start shouting. But in reality, the socialists and workers are shouting because the world is already in chaos!"[49]

As in 1921, today the world is in chaos, and Eroshenko's tales, written over a century ago, continue to have relevance, urging readers, young and old, to think about and act upon the many problems confronting their society. Drawing on what fairy-tale historian Jack Zipes has observed as the "subversive potential" of fairy tales, Eroshenko transforms his seemingly innocent narratives of plants, animals, and children into provocative commentaries that expose the exploitation, racism, and hypocrisy at the core of Western civilization. Of course, he was not alone in this effort, but rather was joined by countless men and women in the United States, Britain, Germany, India, Japan, China, and elsewhere, who, in different contexts, turned to children's literature as a tool for raising the consciousness of the young. Considered in this light, both Eroshenko's life and work speak to a remarkable transnational discourse that took place across the world in the early twentieth century. As it is only in recent years that scholars like Sho Konishi, Andrew F. Jones, and Ian Rapley have identified Eroshenko's important contributions to this discourse, I look forward to seeing how his contributions will be incorporated into the phenomenal scholarship on radical children's literature already put forth by Jack Zipes, Julia Mickenberg, Kimberly Reynolds, Evgeny Steiner, and many, many others.

Importantly, Eroshenko's tales are also a cherished artifact of the world's blind community, offering a unique and often-neglected perspective to the fairy-tale genre. Writing on the theme of disability as it appears in the ubiquitous fairy-tale "quest narrative," author and disability rights activist Amanda Leduc astutely observes: "In fairy tales . . . disability often operates as an impetus back toward balance and the world of the ideal; if the disabled narrator can only successfully complete the quest, do what is required of them, and learn, their disability will be lifted from them and they'll occupy an abled space in the world once more."[50] When Eroshenko writes of disability in his tales—be it physical or psychological—he often subverts this quest narrative, presenting the argument that individual action is not enough to set the world right: collective action is required. Although he rarely depicts any character succeeding in the world, he makes it plainly and painfully clear that their tragic fates are undoubtedly due to the fact that society has failed to imagine their full participation.

Only in "An Eagle's Heart" does Eroshenko fully upend the ableist quest narrative, presenting disfigurement not as a symbol for disability but for superhuman ability. In the tale, a falconer captures two eagle princes, whose parents kidnap his sons as retribution. When after many years the eagle princes and falconer's sons are returned to their respective parents, they are completely changed. In particular, the falconer's sons now exhibit the hard limbs, beak-like noses, and talon-like nails of the eagles who had held them ransom. Rather than being socially ostracized for their differences, the brothers are welcomed back into their community, imbuing it with a fiery revolutionary spirit that one day will allow it to overthrow its oppressors. Meanwhile, the eagle princes, who were socialized according to the limiting norms of human society, lose their pride and sense of freedom.

On a personal note, Eroshenko's tales have served as a reminder to myself, a second-generation Ukrainian Canadian, that my heritage belongs to a diverse and ever-evolving world of liminal boundaries. These tales offer me the rare opportunity to promote a near-forgotten voice from the Ukrainian diaspora—somehow made possible by my ability to read Japanese and Esperanto and despite my inability to read Ukrainian (yet!). Beyond introducing Vasily Eroshenko (or Vasyl Yeroshenko, as his name is pronounced in Ukrainian) to a new audience, I hope this collection will act as a bridge between cultures, generate further interest in émigré literature, and challenge us to think about identity in new and interesting ways.

A NOTE ON THE COLLECTION

The present collection is intended to provide an overview of Eroshenko's engagement with the fairy-tale form, with particular emphasis given to tales in which he employed subversive techniques and experimental prose styles to provoke and raise the political consciousness of his readers. Each tale has been selected for the various social and political injustices they highlight, the experimental techniques they exhibit, and the value they have as biographical or historical commentary. Some important tales like "The Land of Rainbows," "The Ferry of Happiness," and "The Wound of Love" have not been included, as the themes they explore are better expressed elsewhere; others like "The First Treasure" or "The Triplets" employ images and language that are not at all acceptable and are, in my opinion, failed works with little subversive potential; last, some tales have not been included because of the state of incompleteness engendered by twentieth-century censorship laws particular to Japan. As Heather Bowen-Struyk and Norma Field explain in their anthology of Japanese proletarian literature, *For Dignity, Justice, and Revolution*, "Since postpublication banning was the predominant form of censorship during the early twentieth-century, editors and authors worked hard to avoid this costly outcome by pre-emptively censoring their texts, using mostly Xs, ellipses, and sometimes Os in place of words that risked running afoul of the authorities."[51] Because tales like "The Young Angel's Mistake" and "The Soul of the Universe" are severely mangled by this type of obfuscation, they have been left out. Perhaps space can be made for more tales, speeches, essays, and Eroshenko's play "Peach-Colored Clouds" in a future collection.

Furthermore, just how many of Eroshenko's unusual tales were originally written in Japanese remains unclear. In this collection, the semi-autobiographical "Some Pages from My School Days," "The Mad Cat," and "Tales of a Withered Leaf," as well as the two prose poems included in the appendix, provide the Esperanto versions written by Eroshenko himself. While certainly written in Japanese, "The Tragedy of the Chick," "Father Time," and "The Red Flower" have survived only by way of Lu Xun's meticulous Chinese translations.

In his autobiography *The Straight Green Path*, Eroshenko scholar Takasugi Ichirō remarks on some of the difficulties in compiling a collection of Eroshenko's works, chief among them being that "while Eroshenko had an excellent understanding of Japanese, we must not forget that it was imperfect."[52] Compounded with this is the fact that his tales received varying degrees of assistance from transcriptionists. Although some of the tales appear quite polished, others not only contain typographical errors but also awkward syntax. With this in mind, I have pulled from a variety of sources to create my translations, including the original Sōbunkaku edition of *Songs Before Dawn* (1921), Lu Xun's Chinese translations, Takasugi Ichirō's *Collected Works of Eroshenko*, volumes 1–3 (1959), Miyamoto Masao's Esperanto translations in *A Narrow Cage* (1981), and Eroshenko's own Esperanto writings. Perhaps more than any other translator of Eroshenko's work, I have been quite liberal with my edits while endeavoring to convey Eroshenko's lyrical voice and impassioned political messages.

This collection features two parts: part I includes tales that Eroshenko wrote in Japan (1915–1921) and part II includes tales that he wrote in China (1921–1923). Several semiautobiographical pieces and prose poems also appear in the appendix to this collection, which I hope paint a picture of Eroshenko's character and the world he lived in.

NOTES

1. Vasily Eroshenko, "Unu paĝeto en mia lerneja vivo," in *Lumo kaj ombro*, ed. Mine Yoshitaka (Toyonaka: Japana Esperanta Librokooperativo, 1979), 5.
2. Eroshenko, "Unu paĝeto en mia lerneja vivo," 17.
3. Eroshenko, "Unu paĝeto en mia lerneja vivo," 6.
4. Tatiana Novikova, "Pri la ekspozicio de la Eroŝenko-Domo-Muzeo en Obuĥovka," in *Vivis, vojaĝis, verkis—Ikita, tabishita, kaita—Esearo omaĝe al Vasilyj Eroŝenko, 1890–1952—Eroshenko seitan 125-shūnen kinen bunshū*, ed. Shibayama Junichi, trans. Anatolo Sidorov and Julia Patlan (Tokyo: Japana Esperanto-Instituto, 2015), 7.
5. L. L. Zamenhof, as quoted in *Esperanto: Language, Literature, and Community*, ed. Humphry Tonkin, trans. Humphry Tonkin, Jane Edwards, and Karen Johnson-Weiner (Albany: State University of New York Press, 1993), 23.
6. Zamenhof, as quoted in *Esperanto: Language, Literature, and Community*, 35.
7. Eroshenko, "The Woman and Her Mission," *Beijing nüzi gaodeng shifan zhoukan* (December 3, 1922), 8.
8. Eroshenko, "La unua eksterlanda vojaĝo," in *La kruĉo da saĝeco*, ed. Mine Yoshitaka (Toyonaka: Japana Esperanta Librokooperativo, 1995), 68.
9. Sho Konishi, *Anarchist Modernity: Cooperatism and Japanese-Russian Intellectual Relations in Modern Japan* (Cambridge, MA: Harvard University Press, 2013), 258.
10. Konishi, *Anarchist Modernity*, 260.
11. Shōzō Fujii, *Eroshenko no toshi monogatari: 1920-nendai Tōkyō, Shanhai, Pekin* (Tokyo: Misuzu shobō, 1989), 4.
12. Fujii, *Eroshenko no toshi monogatari*, 8.
13. Eroshenko, "Shizukana minato de," in *Eroshenko zenshu*, vol. 2, rev. ed., ed. Takasugi Ichirō (Tokyo: Misuzu shobō, 1974), 306.
14. Kokkō Sōma, *Mokui—Meiji, Taishō bungaku kaiso* (Tokyo: Hōseidaigaku shuppankyoku, 1982), 285.
15. Konishi, *Anarchist Modernity*, 331. Another invaluable piece of English-language scholarship on this generation of writers is Elizabeth M. Keith's dissertation on the history of *Akai tori* and its editorial policy. See Elizabeth M. Keith, *Dōshinshugi and Realism: A Study of the Characteristics of the Poems, Stories and Compositions in Akai Tori from 1918 to 1923* (PhD diss., University of Hawai'i, 2011).

16. Heather Bowen-Struyk and Norma Field, eds., *For Dignity, Justice, and Revolution: An Anthology of Japanese Proletarian Literature* (Chicago: University of Chicago Press, 2016), 189.

17. Writing for *La Revuo Orienta* in 1930, Hiraoka Noboru pointed to Eroshenko's influence on the next generation of left-wing writers: "I believe there will come a day when the significance of his work on Japan's modern proletarian literature and Japanese literature in general will be recognized." See Hiraoka Noboru, "Washirii Eroshenko," in *La Revuo Orienta*, no. 3 (March 1930), 76.

18. Konishi, *Anarchist Modernity*, 287.

19. Pulled from quotes by Eguchi Kan, Kato Kazuo, and Hasegawa Nyozekan in *Eroshenko zenshu*, vol. 3, ed. Takasugi Ichirō (Tokyo: Misuzu shobō, 1959), 162, 164–165, 247.

20. Hasegawa Nyozekan in his introduction to Eroshenko's third collection of fairy tales, *Jinrui no tame ni* (Tokyo: Tōkyo kankkōsha, 1924). Translated in *Stranga Kato*, ed. Mine Yoshitaka (Toyonaka: Japana Esperanta Librokooperativo, 1983), 3

21. Fujii, *Eroshenko no toshi monogatari*, 22–24.

22. Perhaps to avoid censorship, authors occasionally portrayed Eroshenko under different names, such as "Danchenko" or "Ivan." In such cases, the use of an epithet like "the blind poet" or "the blind musician" made it plainly clear who the "fictional" character was modeled after.

23. Fujii, *Eroshenko no toshi monogatari*, 27.

24. Quoted in *Eroshenko zenshu*, vol. 3, 245–246.

25. Fujii, *Eroshenko no toshi monogatari*, 29.

26. Quoted and recast from Andrew F. Jones, *Developmental Fairy Tales: Evolutionary Thinking and Modern Chinese Culture* (Cambridge, MA: Harvard University Press, 2011), 151.

27. Jones, *Developmental Fairy Tales*, 159–160.

28. Jones, *Developmental Fairy Tales*, 154.

29. Quoted in Julia Lovell's introduction to *The Real Story of Ah-Q and Other Tales of China: The Complete Fiction of Lu Xun*, trans. Julia Lovell (London: Penguin Books, 2009), xix.

30. Jones, *Developmental Fairy Tales*, 150–151.

31. Quoted and recast from Jones, *Developmental Fairy Tales*, 159.

32. According to an official report, he was greeted at the train station by a large crowd of students. Shōzō, *Eroshenko no toshi monogatari*, 93.

33. Lu Xun, *The Real Story of Ah-Q*, 144.

34. Zhou Zuoren, "Eroshenko kun wo omou," in *Jibun no hatake*, trans. Nakajima Osafumi (Sōyushoya, 2019), 93.

35. Eroshenko, "Rakontoj d velkinta folio," in *Lumo kaj ombro*, ed. Mine Yoshitaka (Toyonaka: Japana Esperanta Librokooperativo, 1979), 38.

36. Shi Chengtai, "Eroŝenko en Ĉinio," in *Cikatro de amo*, trans. Shi Chengtai and Hu Guozhu, ed. Mine Yoshitaka (Toyonaka: Japana Esperanta Librokooperativo, 1996), 79.

37. Dongyoun Hwang has observed that Eroshenko's views on the failures of Soviet-style communism particularly influenced the thinking of Yi Jeonggyu, Jeong Hwaam, and other Korean anarchists based in China. See Dongyoun Hwang, *Anarchism in Korea: Independence, Transnationalism, and the Question of National Development, 1919–1984* (Albany: State University of New York Press, 2016), 26.

38. Xiaoqn Xu, *Cosmopolitanism, Nationalism, and Individualism in Modern China: The Chenbao Fukan and the New Culture era, 1918–1928* (Lanham, MD: Lexington Books, 2014), 75.

39. Xu, *Cosmopolitanism, Nationalism, and Individualism*, 73.

40. Ba Jin, "Antaŭparolo al Ŝipo de feliĉo," in *Cikatro de amo*, trans. Shi Chengtai, 102.

41. Lin Yutang, *My Country and My People* (New York: Reynal & Hitchcock, 1935), 285.

42. Quoted in Takasugi Ichirō, ed., "Eroshenko no shōgai," in *Eroshenko zenshu*, vol. 3 (Tokyo: Misuzu shobō, 1959), 225–226.

43. Eroshenko, "La trimova ŝakproblemo," in *El vivo de la ĉukĉoj*, ed. A. Masenko and A. Pankov (Moscow: Impeto–Ruthenia, 1992), 28.

44. Brigid O'Keeffe, *Esperanto and Languages of Internationalism in Revolutionary Russia* (London: Bloomsbury, 2021), 281–282.

45. Anatolij Masenko, "Vasilyj Eroŝenko kaj Esperanto," in *Vivis, vojaĝis, verkis—Ikita, tabishita, kaita—Esearo omaĝe al Vasilyj Eroŝenko, 1890–1952—Eroshenko seitan 125-shūnen kinen bunshū*, ed. Shibayama Junichi (Tokyo: Japana Esperanto-Instituto, 2015), 21.

46. Nikolaj Osipenko, "Esplor-agado pri Vasilyj Erosxenko en Asxhxabad (Turkmenio)," *Ligo internacia de blindaj esperantistoj* (October 30, 2018), http://www.libe.slikom.info/Erosxenko-Konkurso/Nikolaj%20Osipenko%20(Rusio).htm.

47. Eroshenko, "La problem de la internacia rialto," in *Lumo kaj ombro*, ed. Mine Yoshitaka (Toyonaka: Japana Esperanta Librokooperativo, 1979), 81.

48. Eroshenko, "Nova spirito en la mondo," in *Stranga kato*, ed. Mine Yoshi-taka (Toyonaka: Japana Esperanta Librokooperativo, 1983), 71. Eroshenko predicted a war between Japan and the United States in his political fairy tale "Onchō no ranpi" (Wasted Grace). See Eroshenko, "Onchō no ranpi," in *Eroshenko zenshu*, vol. 3, ed. Takasugi Ichirō (Tokyo: Misuzu shobō, 1959), 276.

49. Quoted in *Eroshenko zenshu*, vol. 3, 248.

50. Amanda Leduc, *Disfigured: On Fairy Tales, Disability, and Making Space* (Toronto: Coach House Books, 2020), 196.

51. Bowen-Struyk and Field, *For Dignity, Justice, and Revolution*, 12.

52. Takasugi Ichirō, *Hitosuji no midori no komichi: Eroshenko wo tazuneru tabi* (Osaka: Riveroj, 1997), 174.

PART I

Japanese Tales (1915–1921)

Chapter One

THE TALE OF THE PAPER LANTERN

SHE LIT ME with her love, and lined me with the words, *I love you only*. Indeed, her love was life itself, and brightly did I shine by it.

I watched the people come and go in fine kimonos, paper lanterns in their hands, smiling from ear to ear, like the good god Ebisu. How happy they looked! Some rode in boats while others danced upon the shore. Some beat on drums while others played the shamisen. They seemed to be celebrating something. But what?

It dawned on me. Of course, they were celebrating my birthday! So I burned brighter, much brighter than before. Of all the paper lanterns out that night, my light was the most handsome, and the most mysterious also. Everywhere I went the people smiled to see me, recalling lost days of youth; and in my light did even ordinary words become imbued with deeper meaning. Ah, how wonderful is the light of love!

She sat in a boat and gazed at the Moon.

"The light of this lantern has more meaning than you," she murmured.

"Any light can have meaning in the dark," said the Moon with a frown, and she hid herself behind a cloud of grey mist.

"I wonder," laughed the Waves as they rolled in the sea. But what did they know? They are such fickle things.

"The first time I saw him was in Ueno Park," she said, looking down at me. "He was with some foreigners who had come to watch the cherry blossoms fall. But he was not watching the cherry blossoms fall. His eyes were closed. And as I watched him, I wondered, 'What is he thinking about? And why does he look so weary, as if he has no desire to watch the blossoms?' I pondered this until I had forgotten all about the cherry blossoms, until I was looking only at him. And when he passed me, I said to him, 'Today I found something more interesting to watch than the cherry blossoms'; and he turned and looked at me strangely."

As she spoke, she paid no heed to the beautiful boats all covered with flowers, nor to the festive music that was filling the air.

She watched only me.

"One night," she went on remembering, "he came to the teahouse with his friends. And like before, he seemed to have eyes for nothing. How curious, I thought, and sang to him my very best song. Then, when his face brightened, I knew that he loved me."

Whether she had said this to make me jealous, I cannot say. All that I know is that true love takes no joy in jealousy.

"He came to the teahouse now and then. And whenever he heard me flirting with the other customers, his face would darken. Yet he never once looked at me. Had he taken one look, he would have seen everything. But then he was a strange man. How else to describe him? There are many strange men in this world . . .

"I dropped a violet at his feet.[1] He took no notice of it. Then, when his friends called me over, I declined, saying that I had another customer. I was lying, of course. But he had ignored me. Later, I heard him say that if he could not find work, he would have to return to his own country. As I came near, he turned to me and said, 'I may be going home, but my happiness will remain here.' Still, he did not look at me. Why?

"Little lantern, little lantern, you see that boat over there? The man I told you about is on it now. He is waiting for my answer. You must tell him everything!"

She turned to her boatman.

"Good sir," she begged him, "pray pull up to that boat full of foreigners. I should like to give one of them this lantern."

So we came to the boat, and with trembling hands, she relinquished me to someone on board, saying, "Give this to him."

"To me?" said a pale-faced man.

"To thee," she smiled, and ordered her boatman to steer her away.

The man brought me close, hiding his face from the others.

"Little lantern, little lantern" he whispered, "what did she ask you to tell me?"

---

[1] Author's note: In the language of flowers, a violet means, "Think of me."

"My light," I said proudly, "is lit by her love, and has more meaning than the light of the Moon. She has asked me to tell you that she loves me only."

"I see," said the man. "So it's you that she loves. So she loves the light only, and only what is bright. And to her, the near light of a paper lantern has more meaning than the distant light of the cloud-covered Moon."

I felt his tears on my flame, and nearly extinguish it. But a moment later, I was burning as brightly as before. Surely the light of love cannot be extinguished by tears alone!

She sat in her boat and gazed at the Moon.

The boat full of foreigners pulled up beside her.

"How heartless!" they shouted, and threw me in her face.

"No," said the man. "I should thank you for your honesty." And he ordered his boatman to take him to the big ship that was about to depart for a faraway land.

She leaned over and wept.

Oh, why did she weep?

"Alas! It's over. He loves me not," she sobbed into the water. "My violet meant nothing to him. But then why did his face darken when I flirted with the others? And why did it brighten when I sang to him my songs? And why did he ask me to give him an answer? Did he toy with me only because I am a geisha?"

"I wonder," laughed the Waves as they rolled in the sea.

But she did not hear them. She only wept.

Oh, why did she weep? I was lit by her love, was I not?

"Pray," said the boatman to another who was just then returning from the big ship, "was there a blind man on your boat?"

"Indeed, there was."

She looked up. "What! Where?"

"There," said the boatmen, pointing to the ship.

I felt myself being thrust into the night.

"He was blind?" she exclaimed, raising me higher. "He was blind?"

Chapter Two

THE SAD LITTLE FISH

I

It was a cold and bitter winter. How awful it was for the fish in the pond! The ice was thin when first it formed, but with each passing day had grown thicker, till it loomed fairly above their heads. So the koi and the carp and the loaches all held a meeting to try to come up with a solution. But nothing, it seemed, could be done, for the ice was assailing them from above. In the end, the fish adjourned the meeting, clinging fast to the hope that it would soon be spring, and each swam home with a heavy heart.

Now there lived in the pond a family of carps—a husband and his wife and their son, whose name was Little Carp.

On the night of the meeting, Little Carp could not sleep at all.

"It's cold! It's cold!" he wept again and again.

Ah! But there are no fireplaces or stoves at the bottom of ponds, nor are there warm blankets to crawl under, or thick pajamas to bundle up in.

His mother was sick with worry, there was nothing that she could do to comfort him.

"Hush, my darling," she cooed, and cradled him between her fins, "Soon it will be spring."

"When?" sobbed Little Carp, looking up at her.

"Soon," murmured his mother.

"Really?" said Little Carp. "How do you know?"

"Because it comes every year."

"What if it doesn't come this year?"

"It will come . . ."

"How can you be sure?" asked Little Carp; but his mother did not answer, so he went on: "Old Mister Koi says that if spring doesn't come, we shall die. Is that true?"

"Yes, my darling, it is true."

"Mother, what is 'death'?"

"Death is what happens when you fall asleep forever, when your body stops moving and you no longer feel hungry or cold. Then, your soul will depart for a faraway kingdom, to live in peace and happiness. In that kingdom, there is a big and beautiful pond, where no winter comes, and every day is as warm as a spring day."

"Oh, Mother," cried Little Carp, "is there really such a place?"

"Of course there is!"

"Then we should go there!"

"No," said his mother. "Not while we are alive."

"Why not?" asked Little Carp. "Don't you know the way?"

"I do not," answered his mother.

"Then we should look for it!"

"But that kingdom is for the dead."

"Then we must die!"

"You mustn't say that!"

"Oh, pooh!" shouted Little Carp at the top of his voice. "I don't want to live in this pond!" And he threw a great tantrum right then and there.

So much noise did he make that Old Mister Koi, who lived next door and was a terribly poor sleeper, rushed over to see what was the matter.

"Ah!" he said finally, after the situation was explained to him. "If it is to heaven you wish to go, then you must keep the commandments of the Lord and swim in his ways."

"And what are his commandments?" asked Little Carp.

"His commandments," said the old koi, "are that you honor your parents and your elders; that you love your neighbors, be they in the pond or on land; and that you study hard, so that you might grow up to be a good and righteous fish. Do these things and the Lord will surely call on you to live in his glorious kingdom."

So from that day forward, no matter how cold or tired he felt, Little Carp just smiled and waited for spring to arrive.

II

Well spring did arrive; and when it did, nowhere was there to be found a kinder, more intelligent fish than Little Carp—not in the pond, nor in the neighboring rivers. And no one was better loved, so that even the lusty koi and lovely loaches, who were older in years, took him wherever they went.

As it was spring, and small tributaries were flowing into the pond from every direction, the older fish thought it a good opportunity to introduce Little Carp to the distinguished masters of the surrounding area.

Among them was a long-eared monk, Master Rabbit, who practiced a strict vegetarian diet. Then there were the composers, maestros Bush Warbler and Cuckoo, who had just returned from their winter retreats, and whose feathers were as clear as crystal. These masters found Little Carp to be exceptionally bright and showered him with praise and filled his head with stories of life on land. And of all the stories that Little Carp heard, nothing gave him greater pleasure than those which were about human beings.

Everyone agreed that their brothers and sisters the humans were the most noble and intelligent creatures in the whole world, concluding that while foxes may make great politicians; monkeys, great entertainers; parrots, great linguists; crows, great sociologists; and owls, great astronomers—human beings outshone them all.

And while some remarked that humans were slower on foot than other land creatures, they nevertheless could ride horses and had invented many a curious device to help them move faster, such as cars, trains, and bicycles. Likewise, while humans were admittedly poor swimmers, and certainly couldn't fly, they possessed fire-breathing fish and broad-winged birds that allowed them to move freely through water and air.

The humans were marvelous indeed!

Little Carp could listen to this talk forever, each new anecdote fanning the flames of his desire to make human contact.

III

It was a wonderful spring indeed. Every morning maestros Bush Warbler and Cuckoo traded solos over a choir of wasps and honeybees, while butterflies turned somersaults in the air; and every evening the frogs gathered for lively poetry readings and lectures that lasted long into the starry night. Sometimes Little Carp took part in these readings, and in his own innocent way spoke poetically on the kingdom of God.

"So love thy neighbor as thyself and be happy," he often concluded, "and thee shall gain entrance to a greater, more beautiful kingdom: a kingdom without cold or hunger, or any inconvenience whatsoever, where a fish may walk upon the earth or fly across the sky, and a bird may swim beneath clear waters!"

Before long the kingdom of God and all that it represented was showing up as motifs in songs, dances, speeches, and poetry. Everyone quoted Little Carp's sermons, even the creepy crawly things that generally lived apart from society.

And in the evening, when the faraway church-bell began to toll, the fish would rise up to the top of the water, and the frogs would sit down on their logs, and the butterflies would alight on the flowers, to listen, for it was said that the bell was being rung for the birds in the trees and the fish in the waters and the insects in the grass, and that the humans were praying for the peace and prosperity of all things. So the creatures in the pond prayed too:

for the happiness of their human brothers and sisters; and their prayers, smelling of wildflowers, and glittering in the golden rays of the setting sun, rose silently to God in his kingdom.

Now the Pastor of the church had a son who, like Little Carp, was bright and well-behaved, and admired by everyone. He even had a little dog who spoke highly of him whenever he came down to the pond for to take a drink of water. And the more that Little Carp heard about this boy, the more desirous he grew to befriend him.

IV

One day there arose a commotion at the edge of the pond. When Little Carp swam over, he found some frogs engaging in what appeared to be a heated argument.

"Is everything all right?" he asked, and the frogs told him that the venerable Master Rabbit had been sitting in quiet meditation when the Pastor's Son suddenly leapt out and, grabbing him by his two long ears, whisked him away.

Little Carp gasped. But before he could speak, Miss Swallow flew down to inform the group that Maestro Bush Warbler had been captured also. Apparently, he had been so engrossed in a composition that he was caught off-guard.

Nobody knew what to do or say.

Then, a few nights later, when the frogs were holding their monthly poetry workshop—there was a full-moon, and they agreed that in spite of the recent abductions, it would be wrong to go to sleep without paying tribute to the Moon Goddess—the

Pastor's Son appeared yet again, and carried off the most celebrated member of the group!

Rumors circulated till dawn. Nobody slept a wink. And in the morning, all the creatures assembled to discuss what was to be done about the human child who was wreaking havoc on their once peaceful community.

Little Carp attended the meeting with his parents. He felt that his world had been cast in shadow, and nothing at all made sense.

"Why does the Pastor's Son torment us?" he asked.

"Human beings may be marvelous creatures," answered his father; "but sometimes they get up to no good. And there is nothing more wicked than a human child. Soon enough, the banks of this pond may be lined with children bearing hooks and nets, each looking to cause us all a lot of grief with their pranks."

"But if they do that," cried Little Carp, "how will they get to the kingdom of God? There must be something that we can do to help them!"

But before he had finished speaking these words, Miss Butterfly arrived, fluttering here and there like a wind-blown leaf. She was dreadfully pale, and her golden wings and black antennae shook with abject fear.

A crowd formed beneath her, and everyone asked what on earth was the matter. After she had calmed down a little, she seated herself upon a flower petal, took a deep breath, and began to speak.

"It was a lovely morning," she began. "The wasps, who had all the day to themselves, had made plans to visit the Pastor's garden. All the garden was in bloom, awash with reds and whites and yellows. There were flowers everywhere, growing between the trees and in the flowerbeds, and all the insects seemed to be drunk on the sweet smell of nectar. So happy were the wasps that in their singing and dancing, nearly all of them had forgotten, if only for a moment, the troubles that had recently upended their world. Oh! But then the Pastor's Son appeared with his net, and whisked a whole swarm of them away."

The news of this most recent abduction agitated the crowd, but after much discussion, it was decided that as soon as the church-bell began to toll, Miss Butterfly should hasten to the church and ask the congregation to reign in the Pastor's son.

Evening came, and tensions were high. None of the creatures who had gathered dared to return to their hole or nest. All that they could do was stare at each other in silence and wait for Miss Butterfly to return.

After a while, she came back, and looked to be on the verge of tears.

All at once did everyone feel their heart shrink to the width of a lotus-flower fiber.

"Lies, all lies!" cried Miss Butterfly as she landed on a flower. "We will never be welcomed into the kingdom of God."

"Why not?" wondered the crowd.

"Because," said Miss Butterfly, "we have no soul. Only human beings have souls, so only they will be welcomed into the kingdom of God."

Panic-stricken voices rose up one after the other—

"You must be mistaken!"

"Perhaps you misheard them!"

"No," answered Miss Butterfly; "for so it is written in the Book of the Lord."

"Then where are we supposed to go?"

"It would appear," said Miss Butterfly, "that we were put on this earth for no other reason than to bring delight to human beings and to nourish them with our flesh." And she looked down on the crowd below, her big sad eyes full of pity and love; and awakening to the pain in her limbs, and to that of her broken heart, she fell down and died.

Put on this earth for no other reason than to nourish our human brothers and sisters!

The crowd bemoaned their fate.

Unable to contain their rage, the angry young koi yelled out, "Nonsense!" and leapt into the air as if to confront God himself, while the gentle loaches fainted, some of them sinking down to the very bottom of the pond.

Miss Butterfly had performed a selfless act, and now she was dead. Needless to say, her funeral was a solemn affair, and there was general weeping throughout. The wasps played a dirge, the warblers sang a threnody, and Mister Mole dug a small grave.

Everyone felt terribly lonely.

"How sad!" they all sighed to each other, "to live one's life as the property of man!" and each went their own way home.

V

Once home the koi and the loaches and the frogs spent the rest of the night in tears. When day broke, no one came out to greet the sun.

Little Carp was overcome with grief. Having lost all faith in the world, he swam listlessly along a deserted edge of the pond, when all of a sudden the Pastor's Son appeared and waded into the water with his net.

"So he's come for more!" thought Little Carp, his body shaking with rage. He felt as though he were on fire, and began to thrash about in the water.

"Take me!" he cried, swimming into the net, "take me before you take the others, for I could not bear to watch you kill them, and would rather you kill me first!"

The Pastor's Son ran home, laughing, and placed Little Carp on his desk.

Little Carp looked round the room. On the walls hung the skins of Maestro Bush Warbler and Master Rabbit, while on the desk lay their white bones. In a glass case were arranged rows of butterflies, old friends of his, pins piercing their hearts. And straight ahead, on a small tin tray, was the freshly dissected corpse of the celebrated frog poet who had been kidnapped the night before. His open heart twitched eagerly for Death.

In the face of these horrors, Little Carp found it impossible to breathe. He wanted to scream, but he couldn't, his jaws were too stiff to open. All that he could do was flap himself against the desk again and again.

A short while later, the Pastor's Son dissected Little Carp.

When he removed the heart, he saw that it was broken. He asked his parents as to how this could be, but received no answer.

How could they know that the fish was too sad?

Years went by, and the Pastor's Son grew up to be a famous biologist. But by then the pond had become incredibly small.

There were few frogs and fish left in it, and no flowers or grasses ever grew there again. In the evenings, when the faraway church-bell tolled, no creatures came out to listen.

■ ■ ■

As for myself, I have stopped going to church. And I do not care to pray to a god who has decreed that all things should serve to nourish and entertain the human race, nor do I believe that such a god even exists.

Chapter Three

THE SCHOLAR'S HEAD

THERE ONCE was a scholarly young mouse who spent an entire day devouring the books that lined the bookshelves of an eminent Politician's study.

When at last the evening came, he felt tired.

"Ah! Science is a taxing thing," he sighed, "for mice and men alike!" and he leaned back on the Politician's couch in a manner most scholarly.

From a hole in the wall, there watched a crowd of anxious mice. They were surprised to see the Scholar sitting so comfortably on the couch.

"You can't sit there!" they shouted.

"Why not?" said the Scholar. "I am taking a break from my studies."

"On the couch?" they exclaimed. "Has the Cat gone to see his wife?"

"Who cares?" replied the Scholar. "My concern is the world." And he frowned as if he were struggling with some very important truth.

When they heard this, the other mice wondered if the world were not on the verge of some terrible calamity, and they put their heads further out of the hole.

"What do you mean, *the world*?"

"You poor ignorant creatures!" cried the Scholar. "If only you would open up a book, what shocking discoveries you would make, like how the earth moves, or rather *spins*—"

"Oh, hush!" interrupted a middle-aged Mouse-Wife, "you mustn't say such things! You will only get yourself in trouble. Why, I heard that years ago they set fire to some stupid human being—they called him Giordano Bruno, I think—for making such a reckless claim. And then just the other day, they set fire to that poor mouse whose mother lives next door to kitchen, for the very same reason, no doubt!"

"Nothing of the kind," said the Scholar. "Ask any six-year-old, and they will tell you that the earth spins."

"And no one sets fire to them?" cried the Mouse-Wife.

"Of course not. After all, the earth spins, and that's a fact."

"And why should it do that? Something doesn't add up."

"The other day I heard the cook talking about the high price of kindling," said an eager little mouse from the back of the crowd. "Could that be the reason?"

Now this was a very earnest guess, and the mice in the crowd all nodded their heads together, for there was a great deal of logic in it, but for whatever reason the Scholar continued to show his utter indifference.

"That is beside the point," he said. "The fact remains: the earth is round, and it spins."

"Does that mean we could fall off it?" cried someone.

"This is why I say we should not leave the hole for very long," remarked the Mouse-Wife. "Indeed, there is no safer place than a hole, whether the earth spins or not!"

"Nobody is going to fall off the earth," said the Scholar, and he silenced the crowd with the calm authority of his voice, "not us mice, nor any other creature. Indeed, had you ever nibbled on the contents of a book, you might have learned about a law which states that all objects of a certain mass must fall to earth. In other words, so long as you put on weight, you need not fear falling—except, of course, on your nose."

"I am relieved to hear that!" exclaimed a gray mouse. "But I fear that we do not carry as much weight as we used to. Just look at the humans! Why, they are growing thinner by the day—and I don't just mean their scholars, but their laborers and farmers also. And if anything of theirs has grown, it is only their arrogance and cunning."

"If the humans become too thin," said a young mouse who had lost a part of his ear to a trap the day before; "will they fall into space?"

"I certainly hope so!" replied his neighbor, smiling at the thought. "I wish they would drift far, far away. And if the cats went with them, even better!"

"Nonsense!" shouted the Mouse-Wife. "Why, if not for the humans, where would we get our rice and barley? We would starve to death! And besides, while it may be true that the scholars, farmers, and laborers are getting thinner by the day, the cats and cooks don't seem to be losing any weight at all. So I wouldn't get my hopes up if I were you."

The Scholar had to admit that none of the young mice where quite as prudent as the Mouse-Wife. "Indeed," he said. "Besides, the farmers and laborers will not fall off the earth, no matter how much weight they lose. For the lighter the farmer, the heavier his taxes. And taxes aside, there are still other ways to put on weight. Take meditation. It is a very popular activity among humans, and apparently an excellent way to get fat. Now, seeing as you all have an infinite amount of time, I recommend trying it—only I will not be joining you, there being so many books left to read, and so many important matters to attend to."

But the other mice wanted to hear more.

"What other matters could there be?" they wondered. "If we aren't going to fall off the earth, then what is there to worry about?"

"A far more pressing matter," said the Scholar in a stern tone of voice; and the mice waited for him to continue. They were no doubt unfamiliar with the ancient Chinese saying, "Knowledge is the mother of misfortune."

So as soon as there was perfect silence, the Scholar went on. "The earth," he explained, "is in motion. It is always in motion, for such is the law of the universe. Where is it headed? What path is it on? Nobody knows. But just think: tomorrow—nay, even an hour from now—the world as we know it may collide with some totally unknown object and be destroyed. *That* is my concern. It is the greatest concern of the human race. And the thought of it makes sleeping or eating near impossible, for there is no way to escape the unease that it instills in the mind—save for one way."

At this point the young Scholar's voice began to quiver, and for a moment he paused, his eyes bright with passion. The other mice were hanging on his every word, and were shaking their little tails feverishly.

"And which *way* might that be?"

The Scholar paused again, and there followed an even longer silence, one so quiet that the beating of little mouse hearts could be heard.

"The earth," he continued, "must keep on moving. But in which direction should it move? To the right or to the left, backwards or forwards? This answer has yet to be determined. So we must determine it for ourselves. Now, would it be safer for us to move forward than to turn left? We cannot say, just like we cannot say that it would be any safer for us to turn right. After all, danger is always ahead, whether we are facing forward or left or right. Our only other option, then, is *moving backwards*—Well?"

There followed another silence, one so quiet that even the bristling of little mouse fur could be heard. The Scholar had worked the mice to such a pitch of excitement that their breathing had become loud and uneven.

"Since the dawn of time," he declared, "the path on which our world has traveled has been a safe one. That much is clear. We are all living proof of the fact that while traveling on this path our world has encountered no fatal collision. And so it should be clear that our continued and guaranteed safety lies in the way back!"

At this the silence that had been building up among the mice exploded with a thunderous round of applause. It sounded like the rattle of windowpanes in a rainstorm. The impressionable young mice shouted, "Hear, hear!"; and some of them even rushed over to slap their tails against the legs of the couch on which the Scholar was seated.

"Now then," said the Scholar once the crowd had settled down, "how do we turn the earth around, and by what means? That is the problem of the hour. It is what torments Lloyd George, Clemenceau, and all the great politicians of our time. And until it has been solved, our world will have no rest. I, too, have committed myself to it and believe that it can be solved. And it *will* be solved! Ah, but tonight you should return to your nests, for there are still a few more books that I need to nibble over. I only ask that you remember the mouse scholar who labored day and night to save the world, for your sake and for the sake of all living things!"

When the Scholar had finished speaking, the mice bounded across the floor of the study, leaping and dancing like mad. Indeed, few scholars have ever been treated to such a display of gratitude by the masses, be they members of the genus Mus or the Japanese Empire.

Hearing the ruckus that the mice were making, the Cat, who had hitherto spent the day lazing about one room over, let out an exaggerated yawn, and rose to all fours.

"Inexcusable!" he said, spitting. "Who on earth is making that noise?" And he sauntered into the study, arching his back as he went.

But the study was empty. The mice had all gone back to their hole. Only the young Scholar remained, nibbling over something in the pages of a book.

"Just you wait," said Cat to himself, and he slipped into a corner. "I will punish you!"

The Scholar was nibbling over an academic treatise on imperialism, every page of which seemed to offer up new facts and solutions. His heart raced faster and faster with excitement until, with a dramatic gesture, he leapt off the bookshelf and raced towards the mouse hole.

"Eureka!" he shouted. "I've found it!"

"No," cried the Cat. "I have!" And he pounced out from the corner, landing with his paw on the Scholar's tail. From the hole in the wall there rushed a group of young mice, who upon seeing the Scholar and the Cat all started and turned back—but the way had been blocked by still other mice trying to get out.

One can hardly imagine the chaos made by all those mice in front of the hole. Indeed, it was the one time when few could argue that guaranteed safety lay in the way back.

"Oh!" cried the Scholar. "Great and powerful Master! Let me go! I have made a great discovery. I have discovered a way to turn the world around. Please, for the sake of our planet, for the sake of all creatures, spare me my life!"

But the Cat had been born with a cold heart. "Inexcusable!" he hissed. "The world does not need mice pretending to be scholars. There are plenty of cats to do that"; and he bit off the head that contained *the great discovery*.

"I have nothing against scholars," he went on, grinding the head between his teeth, "but I find that they, or rather their heads, taste funny. They are certainly less tasty than that of your average mouse. Why is that, I wonder? Perhaps this is a matter for us cats to look into."

And so the mouse Scholar died before he could announce his great discovery that would have helped to turn the world around.

Only don't tell Lloyd George and the other world leaders. How terribly sad it would make the lot of them!

Chapter Four

BY A POND

IT WAS EVENING-TIME. The temple bell was tolling. From the Great Hall of the Buddha, the Abbot could be heard intoning a sutra. A kitchen door slid open, and out stepped a young Monk, a bowl of food scraps in his hands. The Monk carried the scraps to the temple pond, where there were many black and bright-colored fish. He fed the fish, and they all rose up to the top of the water, to bask in the evening light and listen to the Abbot reciting the words of the sutra. Far away, the sun, a purple shipwreck on the horizon, was sinking into the golden sea. Autumn cicadas looked on, filling the air with long and wistful cries.

Two small Butterflies, not yet a day old, one with wings of silver, and the other with wings of gold, sat watching the sun sink into the sea.

"What's this!" exclaimed the gold Butterfly. "Surely we cannot live without the sun?"

"It's so cold!" replied his silver companion. "Is there nothing we can do to stop it?"

"Nonsense!" chirped an old Cricket who was in the grass nearby and had overheard the conversation. "There will be a new sun tomorrow."

"Be that as it may," responded the gold Butterfly, "are you not sorry to lose this one?"

"Certainly not," answered the Cricket. "We lose one every day!"

"Isn't that wasteful?" asked the silver Butterfly. "Let us do something about it."

"Don't be ridiculous!" cried the Cricket. "There will be a new sun tomorrow, you hear?"

But the Butterflies had only been born that morning and were unable to follow the logic of the wise and experienced Cricket.

"Even still," mused the gold Butterfly, "it would be a shame to let a good sun go to waste"; and turning to the silver Butterfly, said, "Fly eastward, friend, to the sun that will rise tomorrow, and see if you can persuade it to rise a little earlier. Meanwhile, I shall fly westward, where the present sun is about to set, and there shall try to persuade it to come back."

"What!" there sounded a gruff croak, and a slimy, wet Frog leapt up from the damp embankment. "Who said that? Halt, or I'll eat you! Can't you see that we have enough trouble with the one sun as it is? And you would have two of them at once? Madness! Why, that would surely lead to calls for three, four suns even. I dare say, what you are attempting is nothing short of treason! Treason, you hear me? Now who is it that was spouting such nonsense? Show yourself, fiend, that I may eat you!"

"It wasn't me," said the Cricket, putting his head through the grass. "Personally, I think we should do away with the sun altogether."

"We're sorry you feel that way," said the Butterflies sadly, and bidding the Cricket and the Frog farewell, flew off, one to the east, and the other to the west.

In the distance, the temple bell continued to toll, while the purple shipwreck of sun sank deeper and deeper into the golden waves of the sea. As always, the autumn cicadas looked on, filling the air with long and wistful cries . . .

■ ■ ■

A short while later, a group of Frogs assembled at the foot of an old pine, croaking noisily and making the wildest gestures with their little webbed hands. In the topmost branches of the pine was an administrative office, the Chief Administrator of which was a Brown Wood Owl.

"Your Honor!" cried the Frogs in one voice: "Something terrible has happened!"

"Have you any idea what time it is?" groaned the Owl as he stepped out of the darkness. "It is too early!"

"No, your Honor," responded the Frogs. "It is too late! We are in the midst of a revolt, a most terrible revolt!"

"A revolt!" screeched the Owl. "Are the honey bees on strike again?"

"Worse, your Honor! There is a plot to raise the sun before the night is over!"

"What!" cried the Owl, and his big round eyes nearly popped out of his head. "Why, that would threaten the very existence of this administration, and cause all of my staff to go blind! Who, who, I say, are the rogues of which you speak?"

"A pair of young butterflies, your Honor. One is seeking to raise the sun in the west, and the other the sun in the east."

The Owl started. "Police! Police!" he cried.

There was a rustle of wings, and two sleepy-looking Bats appeared out of the gloom.

"Yes, your Honor?" they yawned.

"A complaint has been lodged against two butterflies," said the Owl. "One is traveling west; and the other, east. You are to apprehend them immediately."

"Yes, your Honor," responded the Bats. "But how shall we identify them?"

"One is silver," shouted a Frog.

"One is gold!" hollered another.

"They have four wings!" cried a third.

The Owl let out a screech. "I expect you to know a rogue when you see one!" he hooted angrily. "Well? what are you waiting for? Hop to it!"

So the Bats flew a short distance into the woods, to discuss the particulars of their entrusted mission.

"We must hurry," said the one to the other, "or we shall never catch up to those Butterflies."

"Do you honestly think we could? No, let us go to the mountain and play."

"But—the rebels!"

"Ha! It is quite clear that you have only joined the force. Let me tell you that come tomorrow there will be plenty of butter-flies about. We will simply round a couple of them up."

"But they will plead innocent!"

"Innocent! Everybody pleads innocent, even when guilty. Now come along, friend. Let us play on the mountain."

■ ■ ■

Early the next morning a group of primary-school Students came down to the sea and found the gold Butterfly lying dead in the surf.

"A dead butterfly!" cried the Students. "Do you think that it drowned?"

"Naturally," answered their Teacher, raising one finger into the air. "That is why I am always telling you that 'danger lies in the deep.'"

"But we want to swim!" cried the Students.

"In that case," replied the Teacher, "you should swim where it is shallow. Indeed, there is no need to swim where it is deep. Swimming is a sport, and when civilized man means to cross a body of water, he does so by bridge or by boat."

At that moment the Monk from the temple passed by.

"And what if the boat capsizes, or the bridge breaks?" he asked.

But the Teacher gave him no answer.

By and by a group of secondary-school Students came along to the spot.

"Look," said their Teacher, pointing instructively to the dead butterfly. "This butterfly grew tired of its life on the island, and tried to fly away. And look what has become of it. Indeed, this is why it is important to knows one's place and to be satisfied with one's possessions."

But the Monk, who was still on the beach, could not find satisfaction in this lesson.

"And what about those who lack both status and possessions?" he asked; and some of the Students snickered outright.

But the Teacher paid him no heed. "Do this," he went on, "and you will bring happiness to yourself and to your country."

Still later, a group of Students from the university arrived.

"Our instincts cannot be trusted," declared their Professor. "Just look at this butterfly. During its lifetime, it knew of nothing but small ponds and streams. Then, imagining the great ocean to be yet another pond, it tried to cross it. And now we bear witness to the consequence, and are reminded that nothing is more valuable in life than experience. In a way, all of you resemble this butterfly, in your eagerness to graduate and go rushing out into the world without any experience to guide you."

"And how are they to gain experience if they are not free?" asked the Monk, who was still standing on the beach.

"Free?" said the Professor. "To be sure, man's desire for freedom is instinctual. But who is to say that his instincts are not misguided?"

■ ■ ■

Years later, the primary-school Teacher was praised for his ped-agogy; the secondary-school Teacher was made the principal of his school; and the university Professor was given a prestigious award for writing a long article with so many words that every-body pretended to understand when, really, they did not.

Meanwhile, the Monk became known to the authorities as a troublemaker.

As for the two Butterflies, who could not bear to watch the world descend into darkness, and who only wanted to save it by calling back the sun . . .

Well, nobody thought anything of them at all.

Chapter Five

AN EAGLE'S HEART

THERE IS no bird more majestic or free than the eagle; no bird more strong or brave; and no creature that takes more pleasure from the high and lonely mountains.

It is the King of Birds.

No man would dare question the strength and bravery of his king or leader. But the eagles do not judge greatness by wing-span alone. They never have. For they know that any one of them may become a king or great leader, and therefore they treat each other with the utmost respect. Indeed, they do not behave like the kings and leaders of man, who force their subjects to engage in stupid wars and other meaningless disputes. Rather, each eagle strives for ever more powerful wings, a fiercer beak, sharper talons and a keener sense of sight; and never do they resort to things like intimidation or flattery.

It is in this sense that eagles have long differed from man. For man has always derived his strength from the oppression of those who are weaker than himself, and having never known true freedom, has always lived in misery.

What an unfortunate creature is man! And yet is it not man who claims dominion over every creeping thing? How ironic!

I

There once was a mountain kingdom that was ruled by its larger, more powerful neighbor. All that the two kingdoms ever did was fight, while on the highest mountain in the land, the eagles lived in peace and happiness.

For tens of thousands of years, the eagles burned with one desire: to reach the sun and bask in its eternal warmth and brightness. For tens of thousands of years, they strived to climb higher and higher each day, holding fast to the belief that their descendants would someday get there. And indeed, after many generations, their wings had grown stronger, carrying them higher than had those of their ancestors.

> The sun is a thing to be loved
> So fly to it, my child!
> Do not go down to the valley below
> Look not on what is there
> The sun, it is a source of strength
> The sun, our Promised Land—
> Do not go down to the valley below
> Look not on what is there
> The earth, it is a narrow cage

A place where slaves go to die—
Do not go down to the valley below
Look not on what is there
It is a world for the faint of heart
The foolish world of man—
Do not go down to the valley below
Look not on what is there

Such was the song that every eagle mother taught her young since time immemorial. One wonders how it must have made them feel, the oppressed people of the mountain kingdom, whenever they heard it being sung!

■ ■ ■

The King of the Eagles had his nest on the loneliest cliff of the tallest mountain in the land, and there he lived with his mate, the Queen, and their two eaglets, the princes.

Every morning the King and Queen took the princes to the cliff's edge and cast them off. Then, seconds before they hit the ground, they caught them and bore them back to the top again. Soon the princes were flying up and down the mountain as though it were nothing at all. When the King and Queen saw this, they were quite pleased and began dropping them from greater heights. At first the princes lost consciousness as they fell, but in time their wings grew stronger, and they could fly back to their nest with ease.

One day the King turned to his mate and said, "Let us drop the eaglets into the valley." So they carried the princes to a great height and dropped them.

The princes flew with all their might; but after a while their wings gave out.

"Help me, brother!" cried the younger Prince; "my strength fails me!"

So the elder Prince put forth his remaining strength, and flew to the aid of his brother, while the King and Queen looked on, clapping their wings in exultation.

All of a sudden, a cloud drifted by, and the princes dropped out of sight. So the King and Queen plunged into the valley. But they were too late. For in trying to save his younger brother, the elder Prince had used up all his strength and had fainted. Now the two brothers lay like stones at the bottom of the valley floor.

When the King and Queen arrived to seize the unconscious bodies of the eaglets, there appeared a mighty Fowler and his two sons, who tried to snare them. The King and Queen fought to retrieve their young, but the Fowler proved too strong, and thinking the princes to be dead, they beat a hasty retreat to the sky.

But the princes were not dead, and awoke upon arriving at the Fowler's cottage home. There the Fowler clipped their wings and gave them to his sons, who, despite being only six and seven years old, took good care of them. The boys lavished much affection on the princes, and took them everywhere—only not to the mountain, for their father forbade it.

When the people heard about the eaglets falling into the valley, they deemed it to be a sign, and were filled with joy. For they believed that the eaglets had come to deliver them from their oppressor, and they implored the Fowler to do everything in his power to make sure that the royals' every need was met.

But before a week had passed, something terrible happened. The Fowler's younger son went missing. His friends described a massive eagle shooting down like a thunderbolt, and seizing the child in its sharp talons. Everybody was shaken. Then, a few days later, tragedy struck twice when the Fowler's elder son went missing also.

The people said much about these tragedies. Only the Fowler said nothing, and continued to see that the princes were well looked after.

At first the princes felt very alone and yearned for their freedom. But because they were loved by the children of the village, they began to grow accustomed to the world that was around them, and even came to love the company of man. And after a time, their only real regret was that they were bound to a tree by an iron chain.

II

Five years went by. On the fifth anniversary of the princes' capture, the Fowler quietly removed their chains and brought them back to the mountain, where he released them. When the people found out, there was a great commotion, in the midst of which the Fowler's missing sons returned from the mountain.

So completely changed were they that none, at first, could recognize them. They were both naked, and had long, flowing hair; their chests were as hard as rock, and their limbs as strong as steel. They had piercing eyes and break-like noses. Their teeth were large as the fangs of a wolf, and their nails were sharp as the claws of a tiger.

The brothers told of how the eagle monarchs had raised them in their nest; of how they had been doted on; and of how each day the King and Queen had borne them on their wings up into the sky, to cast them down and catch them as they fell. Still more wondrous things they told, and all who listened puzzled over what had happened.

The brothers had once been average boys. Now none could match them in any sport, nor display a greater love for freedom and adventure. From the eagles they had learned the art of setting hearts on fire. And when they struggled with the human tongue, they cried like eagles cry, and so gave voice to wordless thoughts.

They taught the people how to sing:

> The sun is a thing to be loved
> So fly to it, my child!
> Do not go down to the valley below
> Look not on what is there . . .

The sons of the Fowler certainly were wonderful, so the people bestowed on them the name of Eagleheart. How hopeful they must have been, the oppressed people of the mountain kingdom, whenever they looked upon these brothers!

III

The King and Queen of the Eagles were glad to have the princes back again. But after they had looked them over, they saw that they were ruined, for their wings and beaks lacked strength, and their eyes and talons were dull. Worst of all, they appeared to be in danger of losing their sense of pride and love of freedom.

So every day the King and Queen worked to bring them back from ruin; and every day the Queen would sing to them in the hope that her song might revive their weakened spirits and inspire them to become proud kings. Indeed, every day for ten years the King and Queen worked to expunge the spirit of man from their hearts; and in the end the children flew higher than their parents and had sharper talons and a keener sense of sight.

But still they lacked an eagle's heart, displaying a weakness all too human. For when they flew towards the sun, they looked down; and when they wheeled in the open air, they seemed distracted; and when they climbed higher than the other eagles, they cried not cries of victory, but cries of lonely yearning for their former lives. They fasted for days on end and often did not hunt; and when they did, they spared the lives of the animals they caught.

How sad the King and Queen must have been to see them acting this way! All of their playmates mocked them and called them "Human-heart"; and often did the King and Queen chide them for the shame they had brought upon their family.

■ ■ ■

One day, when the elder Prince returned from wheeling about the sky, he came before his father, and said: "Oh, Father! 'Tis a silly thing, this ancient belief that we must fly towards the sun! It is no fun at all, and guarantees no happiness. Today I set out on the journey myself, and flew as high as my wings would carry me. But the higher I flew, the colder I became, and the less I was able to see, till at last I was dazzled, and having nearly lost consciousness, fell out of the sky. Truly the sun is a lonesome place, and I shall fly to it no longer!"

On hearing this, the King ruffled his feathers and screeched, "Human-heart!" And flying at the Prince, dug his knife-like talons into his throat. The Prince, who yearned for the uneventful life that had been his in the valley below, let out a shrill cry. But he did not resist, and so he died by the talons of his father.

That same evening, when the younger Prince returned to his nest, he came before his mother, and said: "Oh, Mother! Do not make me fly towards the sun, not when it serves me no purpose! Rather, let me go down to the valley below, to make my nest there in a tree, and live with man and the other animals. We eagles will not find happiness on the sun; for if happiness is to be found anywhere, it will be found in our fellowship with man. Indeed, I know this because I have seen it there myself."

On hearing this, the Queen ruffled her feathers and screeched, "Human-heart!" And flying at the Prince, dug her knife-like talons into his throat. The Prince, who longed for the valley below, and yearned for fellowship with man, let out a shrill cry. But he did not resist, and so he died by the talons of his mother.

Later that night, the King and Queen carried the bodies of the two princes down into the valley and dropped them before the house of the Fowler.

> The sun is a thing to be loved
> So fly to it, my child!
> Do not go down to the valley below
> Look not on what is there . . .

From that day forward, whenever the eagles sang this song, they could not help but think of how the princes had been warned of the dangers that come of a human heart.

■ ■ ■

When morning broke, the bodies of the eagles were discovered, and there was much excitement among the people. For a rebellion was underway, and the Brothers Eagleheart were leading the charge against their oppressors. Such master strategists were they that the enemy had been thrown into complete disarray and seemed to be on the verge of defeat. But now, with the discovery of the dead eagles, the people feared in their hearts that they had seen a sign that the rebellion would end in failure.

The young women of the mountain laid flowers on the bodies of the eagle princes, singing the song taught to them by the Brothers Eagleheart:

> The sun is a thing to be loved
> So fly to it, my child!
> Do not go down to the valley below
> Look not on what is there . . .

And they buried them as if they had been heroes.

IV

In the capital of the neighboring kingdom, every house was decked with bright festoons, and for miles on end there rang the booming of cannonball-salutes, the banging of fireworks and the playing of music for happy people. On the streets, everybody went about in fine clothing, waving little colored flags and laughing.

It was a picture of happiness.

Only the guillotine, which rose up in the largest square, betrayed a certain sadness. Yet the people gathered round it, singing rousing anthems and waiting for something to happen. They shook hands, congratulated each other on their victory over the mountain kingdom and talked of how the Brothers Eagleheart were soon to be executed.

After a while, a wave of whispering voices rolled in from the back of the crowd, and the brothers appeared, escorted by soldiers. Then all conversation ceased, and the square became silent, even as a graveyard. Only the sharp rattle of a military drum could be heard. It went, *ratta-tat-tat, ratta-tat-tat, ratta-tat-tat* over and over . . .

Yet the brothers were smiling, their eyes ablaze with infinite fiery courage, capable of igniting all the hearts of mankind. When at last they had ascended the execution platform, the rattle of the drum ceased. With bated breath, the crowd watched on. Not once did the brothers avert their gaze from the sky.

Suddenly a valiant cry rippled through the air, and scarcely before its echo could resound, two massive eagles, the likes of which no one had seen before, shot down like great thunderbolts, and, seizing the Brothers Eagleheart, shot back into the sky. The crowd watched on in stony silence, and the entire city became silent, even as a graveyard. A moment later, up above, there came the sound of voices singing:

> The earth, it is a narrow cage
> A place where slaves go to die—
> Do not go down to the valley below
> Look not on what is there
> It is a world for the faint of heart
> The foolish world of man . . .

V

That night all was quiet in the mountain kingdom. The rebellion had ended in failure. Women mourned the loss of husbands and sons. Children mourned the loss of fathers and brothers.

It was a very lonely night indeed.

Having heard that the Brothers Eagleheart had been sentenced to execution, everyone gathered before the Fowler's home. There was no telling the depths of their sorrow. Still, some among them found the strength to raise the youngest of their children towards the infinite night sky, and casting a proud glance upon the others, pray that all be blessed with eagle hearts, that they might one day bring salvation to the mountain kingdom.

All was quiet. The stars twinkled softly, and out of the stillness of the night came a reply to their prayer in song.

Do not go down to the valley below
Look not on what is there
The sun, it is a source of strength
The sun, the Promised Land . . .

Chapter Six

LITTLE PINE

THERE ONCE was a funny Old Woman who lived by a certain country village.

Nobody knew how old she was. Some said a hundred, others a hundred and fifty. As for the Old Woman herself—well, she had forgotten long ago. Still, while her age remained a mystery, years of woe and resignation had clearly left their scars on her face.

She lived in a hut at the edge of a wood, and every day went out to pick herbs, which she used to make potions for treating the ailments of the people in the village.

But her life was exceedingly miserable, for all she ever she looked on were ailing bodies, and all she ever listened to were cries of pain and suffering.

How lonely she must have been!

Yet not once did she doubt the mercy of Heaven. "The gods know full well how much we can bear," she used to say to herself, "and have portioned out hardship accordingly."

One day she went out to the wood to pick herbs as usual. When she arrived, she noticed something like a bundle at the foot of an old pine tree. So she went up to it and looked—and lo! there was a baby girl, not more than a day old.

The Old Woman felt so sorry that she took the child home with her and went round the village looking for someone to raise it as their own. But alas, at that time, in that village, there was not one such merciful person.

Even when it became known that the little girl was blind, there was still not one merciful person willing to take her in.

What was the Old Woman to do? She determined to raise the child herself.

After that, whenever the Old Woman went out to pick herbs, she always laid the girl at the foot of the old pine tree.

And each time she did this, the most wonderful thing happened: a gentle breeze began to blow, and pretty little birds came out, and together they lulled the blind girl to sleep.

Indeed, it would seem that at that time, in that village, there was more compassion among plants and animals than among human beings!

While it was said that the Old Woman had merely given the girl a sleeping potion, it was a fact that she always slept right up to when the Old Woman returned.

So everybody called her Little Pine.

■ ■ ■

After Little Pine had learned how to walk, the Old Woman gave her a puppy and a kitten, and told her to love them like a brother and sister. The puppy she called Shaggy, and the kitten she called Marbles, and the three of them got along remarkably well.

It was not long before Shaggy and Marbles worked out that their elder sister was blind and began assisting her in the house and on the road, so that by the time Little Pine was eight years old, she could run errands in the village.

Around this time Little Pine began to make some friends. One of them was the son of a poor woodcutter, a twelve-year-old boy named Makoto; and the other was the daughter of a wealthy landowner, and her name was Hana.

Whenever Little Pine came to her on an errand, Hana would always send her home with candies and fruits, and sometimes even one of her old toys.

Makoto, however, could not give Little Pine any presents, as his family was too poor. Still, he would take her to the wood, to sit beneath the old pine tree, and read her books and tell her all that he had learned in school that day.

Little Pine was a most loveable child; but often did she come home with eyes all red from crying. And whenever she did, the Old Woman asked her: "Did somebody hurt your feelings?"

"No," Little Pine always answered sadly, the tears rolling down her cheeks.

One evening the Old Woman came home to find Little Pine weeping into her pillow.

"Little Pine, Little Pine," she said softly, "did somebody tease you in the village?"

"Oh, Grandmother!" cried Little Pine; "why do people laugh at me for not knowing who my parents are? Shaggy and Marbles don't know who their parents are, yet nobody laughs at them. But they laugh at me—even Hana and Makoto do—all because my parents abandoned me in the wood. Oh, Grandmother! who are my parents?"

"Why," said the Old Woman, "your mother is a magnificent pine, and your father . . ."

"Oh, Grandmother!" interrupted Little Pine; "I am not a child!" and she began to weep sorely; and Shaggy and Marbles wept too.

Then the Old Woman fell silent, and her wrinkled eyes filled with tears.

■ ■ ■

Another time Little Pine asked the Old Woman: "Grandmother, what is light?"

"Why, light is the source of human happiness!"

"And what is happiness?"

The Old Woman said nothing. She had forgotten long ago what it meant to be happy.

"Well," Little Pine went on, "whatever it is, I suppose it never comes to little blind girls"; and she began to weep.

After that Little Pine began complaining of a pain in her chest, and it seemed to the Old Woman that the burden of living had become too great for her little heart to bear.

So she went into the wood and prayed to a statue of Kannon.

"Oh, Kannon, goddess of compassion," she implored, "who is it that portions out suffering? I ask you to tell them to be more careful! And who is it that decides how much pain one can bear? I ask you to tell them to be less careless!"

That night Kannon appeared to the Old Woman in a dream.

"Old woman," said the goddess, "never before did you doubt heaven's mercy, for which you were granted an exceedingly long life. But now you show doubt, and all because Little Pine complains of a pain in her chest. For this, you shall be punished, and henceforth are you forbidden to speak. In fact, should you utter forth one word, your life will be taken from you that very night. But if you can be silent as I ask you to, I shall make you grateful of heaven's mercy."

And with that she vanished and the dream came to an end.

When the Old Woman awoke, she leapt out of bed and offered up a prayer to the goddess. She was now more certain than ever that all things—be they good or bad in appearance—were in fact veiled blessings from Heaven, designed to show mankind the way; and she determined to speak no more.

The people of the village were very sorry to hear that the Old Woman had gone mute, but no one was more sorry than Little Pine.

■ ■ ■

Years passed over. When Little Pine was thirteen years old, she began to feel that life was to be lived in the pursuit of happiness; and she saw that, above all, happiness required love.

Makoto the Woodcutter was now eighteen years old. He cared for Little Pine as he always had, reading her books and telling her stories from his day.

"Oh, Little Pine," he used to say, "there really is no greater happiness than when a man and a woman love each other and become a family. I myself would like to find a meet partner; and though it is true I am poor, it is really not so difficult in this day and age for the son of a poor man to marry a rich man's daughter. After all, I am the son of a skilled woodcutter, and were I to marry into a wealthy family—Hana's family, for instance—I would surely not disappoint. On the contrary, I think I would soon be running the family business! Oh, Little Pine, the next time you go into town on an errand, will you deliver this letter to Hana for me? Think of all the ways that I could help you were I to someday become wealthy."

Whenever Makoto spoke to her this way, Little Pine always answered, "Yes, dear Makoto," "Anything for you, dear Makoto," and smiled at him faintly. But when she came home, she would lie in bed for hours, or fall over the Old Woman's knee and weep.

One morning Little Pine had been exceedingly quiet, though every now and then a lonely smile played upon her lips.

At length she knelt before the Old Woman.

"Grandmother," she pleaded, "you must do something for me"; and putting her lips quite close to the Old Woman's ear, whispered, "you must make me a potion, one that I might give to Hana, so that she will love Makoto as deeply as I love him."

What could the Old Woman do? How could she refuse such an earnest request? So she made Little Pine the potion and watched her walk out the door.

A while later Little Pine came back and knelt before the Old Woman again.

"Grandmother," she said, looking up through sightless eyes— one might have thought that they could see!—"you are the only one who loves me. Indeed, I may never know the happiness of a man and a woman who love each other and become a family. Hana and Makoto live for that happiness, and I thought I might live for it too . . ." But no sooner had she said these words than she began to weep. And Shaggy and Marbles wept too.

"Oh, Grandmother!" she sobbed, "what husband could be happy with a blind wife? And what child, with a blind mother? I am afraid that I shall never be happy. So pity me, and make me a potion, that I might sleep forevermore!"

How sad the Old Woman must have felt at that moment, and how painful it must have been to hear those cries of despair!

"No, Little Pine!" she spoke at last, forgetting all about the promise that she had made to Kannon, and how a single utterance would bring about her death; "it is the same with the blind as it is with the sighted: man will not know true happiness until he is willing to put the love of others ahead of the love of himself."

Perhaps it was a miracle. Perhaps not. But as soon as she had broken her silence, the Old Woman's face, which had long been clouded by years of quiet suffering, steadily began to brighten, until it was actually radiating light.

Little Pine, Shaggy, and Marbles were not the only ones amazed by the transformation. Outside, the villagers assembled, drawn to the light spilling out from the hut.

The Old Woman sat Little Pine on her knee and had Shaggy and Marbles lie at her feet.

"Naught is there in the world or the next more wonderful than Selfless Love," she said in a voice unusually mild and full of compassion. "It is what gives strength to the weak and disadvantaged, and meaning to meaningless lives. With it, even those who once amounted to nothing shall become a great boon to mankind. For it is this Love that fills the most unhappy heart with joy; this Love that brings peace to the most burdened breast; this Love that will be the key to a happiness hitherto unknown unto man. Indeed, until the day when all the world is conquered by Selfless Love, true happiness will be unattainable, to ourselves and to others, no matter how loudly we clamor after it."

As the Old Woman continued on in this high and noble manner, the people wondered and listened to her speak long into the night.

Later, after everyone had gone home, the Old Woman told Little Pine how the goddess Kannon had come to her in a dream and that she was to die that night because of a promise made and broken.

So the two of them kindled incense and offered a heartfelt prayer to Kannon. Then the Old Woman took to bed, chanting the Buddha's name and patiently awaited the arrival of Death.

But Little Pine had secretly come to a very important decision: she had decided to die in the Old Woman's place.

"Grandmother," she asked, "are you sure that Death will come tonight?"

"Certainly," answered the Old Woman. "For the goddess Kannon told me so."

"And where do you think Death will enter from? From the door, or from the window?"

"From the door. But he is Death, is he not? None can tell where he will enter from."

"He must enter from the door," said Little Pine to herself, and she made her bed there; and Shaggy and Marbles slept at her feet.

A few hours before dawn, Death arrived at the Old Woman's hut.

"This is the place," he said to himself, as he made a note in his notebook. "Doubtless the Old Woman who lives here is nearly two hundred years old. How difficult her life must be! And how miserable! She is probably quite thin and small, like a child. Really, sixty years is long enough for a human life. Besides, the old should make way for the young. That is why we must amend the Heavenly Constitution—or nothing will ever move forward."

After that Death entered from the front door, just as Little Pine had hoped.

"The poor creature is blind and feeble now," said Death when he saw her. "Old woman, I am come to take you to a better world. Surely you are tired of this one."

So Little Pine bid Shaggy and Marbles good-bye, and drew her last breath. Then her soul set forth, leaving behind thirteen years of darkness for the light of eternity, and a lonely life of blindness for a life of infinite joy.

The Old Woman awoke to hear Shaggy and Marbles weeping. So she got out of bed and went to the front of the hut.

There she found the lifeless body of Little Pine.

The people of the village were very sorry to hear of Little Pine's passing. But no one was more sorry than Makoto and Hana, who were going to be married and had only just received the blessing of their parents.

A splendid monument to Little Pine was set up at the foot of the old tree where she had been found, for who could forget the gentle breeze that blew there, and the pretty little birds that came out to sing and lull the blind girl to sleep?

After that the Old Woman vanished, though no one knows where to.

It is said that she went to preach the doctrine of Selfless Love and will not return till all the world is conquered by it.

Chapter Seven

A SPRING NIGHT'S DREAM

I

Far, far away, deep within the mountains, there lies a large and lovely lake, with water as smooth and as clear as the polished surface of a mirror. It is a quiet place, unfrequented by those who like to surround themselves with every sort of convenience. Only a Painter and a pale-faced Youth—the former seeking to connect with Nature; the latter seeking to mend his broken heart—used to visit on occasion, to delight in flowers that glistened like teardrops and birdsong as sweet as a lover's kiss, and so take succor from the unseen hands of God.

But the Painter came to prefer his studio to the mountain landscape; and longing to see his female models once more, rolled up his canvases and returned to the capital city in the east; while the pale-faced Youth returned to the bustling port city in the west, hoping to forget his sorrow under the influence of bright street lights and strong-smelling wine. Since they have left, the lake has become devoid of all human presence.

But that is not to say that it has become devoid of life. For every spring it teems with birds and beasts and little flying insects!

There was one spring when the lake looked especially lovely. Yellow waterlilies and pink and white lotus flowers floated dreamily upon the water. And as there were no humans around to catch or tease them, the water-nymphs were free to play with the fish in the lake or couch with the butterflies and the bees among the flowers. The wood-elves danced merry jigs in the moonlight and raced round the lake with the fireflies. Thrilled by the sight of so much Beauty in one place, the creatures all found themselves dreaming the same spring night's dream; and everything was made more beautiful because of it.

II

One warm spring night there flickered along the edge of the lake a handsome young Firefly with wings that shone like diamonds. It was a full-moon night, and the lake seemed to exude such a passionate glow that the Firefly drifted out onto it, and spent a long time gazing at the moon's reflection in the water.

At last he felt his wings grow heavy. "I must get back to the flowers!" he cried, and began to hasten towards the shore. But before he had gone even a little way, he realized that he lacked the strength to get there.

"How sad it is that I should die on such a romantic night!"

Above him there stretched an infinite sky, with a brilliant moon and softly twinkling stars; while below him, on the mirror-surface of the lake, there stretched another infinite sky, with its own brilliant moon and softly twinkling stars, so that whether he looked up or down, all that he could see were two infinitely stretching skies.

"Bright stars! Beautiful Moon! Still more beautiful World! Farewell!"

The Firefly folded his wings and braced himself for the water.

But when he looked down again, he saw a Goldfish coming up from the depths of the lake—though she seemed to be an angel coming down from Heaven.

"Little Firefly," said the Goldfish in a gentle voice; "what ever is the matter?"

"I am tired!" answered the Firefly. "My wings haven't the strength to fly, and so I must leave this beautiful world. Oh, surely the weak of body have no right to live in it!"

"Nothing of the kind!" said the Goldfish, and her voice made silver ripples on the surface of the water. "I have never heard anything more foolish. Why, Beauty and Grace are also a kind of strength. In fact, of all things, brute strength may be the least in importance. Now alight on my back, and I will take you home."

"If it is not too much trouble," said the Firefly, turning red at the Goldfish's kindness, and he alighted on her back.

So the Goldfish started out for the shore.

"You know," she murmured in spite of her shyness, "I have watched you every night, and wondered how I might make your acquaintance. Surely there is no one in the lake who is as beautiful as you are." And she sighed.

"And I have watched you also," said the Firefly. "And in my heart, I yearned for you. Surely there is no one in the air who is as lovely as you are . . ."

The Goldfish and the Firefly spoke no more; but after that night they continued to see each other regularly. In fact, every night they circled the lake, or couched among the bulrushes near the shore, the Goldfish telling of her life in the water, the Firefly of his life in the wood; and together they dreamed a spring night's dream.

■ ■ ■

There was another night.

A Water-Nymph and a Wood-Elf were sailing on two big green lily pads when they happened to pass the Goldfish and the Firefly, who were out on their evening constitutional.

"That Firefly has the most beautiful wings in the world," said the Nymph.

"And that Goldfish, the loveliest scales," said the Elf.

"How handsome you would look with those wings!"

"And were you to wear a crown of those scales, no other fairy could match you in beauty, neither in the lake, nor in the wood."

"I only want beautiful things," murmured the Nymph, "even in dreams."

"As do I," said the Elf. "Awake or asleep, it is all I can think about . . ."

And the two fairies fell silent.

■ ■ ■

There was another night.

The daughter of a rich Nobleman went out from her summer home, and with a bug-cage in her left hand, and a butterfly net in her right, came down to the shore of the lake.

At the same time the son of a poor Farmer arrived along an old country road, with a fishbowl in his left hand, and a fishing rod in his right.

When the Nobleman's daughter saw the Farmer's son, she went up to him and bowed.

"I am the daughter of the Nobleman who owns this land," she said.

"And I am the son of the Farmer who works it," said the boy.

"I often see little boys working on my family's estate."

"And I often see little girls playing in my family's garden."

"I don't think I like little boys."

"And I don't think I like little girls."

"Boys are so vulgar; they are always rough and know nothing of etiquette."

"And girls are so dim; they always speak in such vague terms that one imagines they are talking in their sleep."

"Well, boys are always fighting and arguing with each other; I really cannot stand them!"

"And girls are always thinking about clothes and makeup, which makes me dislike them even more. In fact, I dislike them more than anything!"

For a long time the boy and the girl argued in the shade of the trees by the mirror-lake. From their nests and their beds, the birds and the bees listened to them, and wondered at why the human children argued so.

"Boys are always tearing their clothes," the girl went on, "and getting themselves dirty; and what's more, they smell funny."

"Well, girls are always wearing such flimsy dresses," said the boy. "And they are so pale and weak that they look like Death."

"I would much rather look at a firefly than a boy!"

"And I would much rather look at a goldfish than a girl!"

"Boys! Sometimes I want to slap them!"

"Girls! Sometimes I want to pull their hair!"

There was a brief silence. A cry of cicadas rose from the trees.

"I think that I will put this cage at the south end of my veranda," said the Nobleman's daughter, "facing the low garden fence."

"And I think that I will put this fishbowl at the north end of my veranda," said the Farmer's son, "where there is no fence to obstruct its view."

"I hope I haven't bothered you. Good-bye!"

"Likewise. Good-bye!"

So the two bowed to each other and parted ways, the girl heading off in one direction, the boy heading off in the other.

III

Later that night the handsome Firefly could be seen in a cage at the south end of the Nobleman's veranda; and the pretty Goldfish, in a fishbowl at the north end of the Farmer's veranda. One wonders what thoughts were running through their tiny heads, what feelings were taking hold in their tiny hearts.

Oh, but I am afraid that there are neither words nor images capable of expressing the sadness felt by these poor creatures!

When the Wood-Elf heard what had happened, he could hardly contain himself; and after all had gone quiet, he stole up to the Farmer's veranda.

"My dear Goldfish," he whispered sorrowfully; "you seem to be in a great deal of trouble. And what's more, your beloved now hangs in a cage at the estate across the way."

But the Goldfish made no answer. She was too sad for words, and merely pressed her golden head against the glass and sighed.

"What would you give me," the Elf went on, "were I to free your friend?"

"All that I can give you is my miserable life," said the Goldfish. "But should it prove useful to win my true love's freedom, I will gladly give it to you."

"I don't want your life!" exclaimed the Elf. "But give me those pretty scales of yours, and I will do what I can."

"Please do!" cried the Goldfish. "For should they ensure my true love's freedom, then I shall not miss even one of them. Now take them, all of them, at once, that he might be set free." And she swam up to the surface of the fishbowl.

So the Elf stripped the Goldfish of her pretty scales, and threw them in a sack.

"My dear Goldfish," he said to her, "whatever you do, do not lose hope. For I will think of a way to get you out also"; and he set off for the mansion across the way.

But the Goldfish did not hear him. She had fallen into a swoon, and was laying at the bottom of the fishbowl like a stone.

Just then the Farmer's son awoke.

"Is it me," he said to himself as he rubbed his eyes, "or is there somebody out on the veranda?" and he jumped out of bed and looked.

But there was nothing there, only the shadow of a figure passing through the gate of the Nobleman's estate. Then he looked down at his fishbowl and found the Goldfish shivering and stripped of all her scales.

"How dare she!" he cried. "This is an outrage!"

Meanwhile the Wood-Elf had arrived at the south end of the Nobleman's veranda.

"My dear Firefly," he said, hiding the sack of scales behind his back; "you seem to be in a great deal of trouble. And what's more, your beloved now lies in a fishbowl on the veranda across the way."

But the Firefly made no answer. He was too grieved for words, and merely wrapped his legs around his chest and hid behind his brilliant wings.

"What would you give me," the Elf went on, "were I to free your little friend, and put her back into the lake?"

"All that I can give you is my nightmarish life," said the Firefly. "But should it prove useful to win my true love's freedom, you may take it from me."

"I don't want your life!" exclaimed the Elf. "But give me those brilliant wings of yours, and I will do what I can."

"My wings?" asked the Firefly, and a look of scorn flashed behind in his tear-dimmed eyes. "You want my wings?"

"Yes," answered the Elf, looking away. "I want your brilliant wings."

"I see," said the Firefly in a barely audible voice. "Then take them! You may have them!" And he flew to the door of the cage.

So the Elf stripped the Firefly of his handsome wings, and threw them in a sack.

Just then the Nobleman's daughter woke up.

"Surely," she said to herself as she rubbed her eyes, "there is somebody out on the veranda." And she slipped out of bed and looked.

But there was nothing there, only the shadow of a figure making its way towards the Farmer's cottage. Then she looked down at her bug cage and found the Firefly collapsed and stripped of its wings.

"How awful!" she cried, and she burst into tears.

■ ■ ■

The next evening the lake gave off a passionate glow. All was quiet, save for the twittering of birds and the humming of honeybees. Having received one last kiss from the sun, the water lilies closed up their petals and went to sleep.

On a large lily pad lay the Firefly, stripped of his brilliant wings. Beside him lay the Goldfish, half submerged in the water.

"I'm cold," whispered the Goldfish. "I haven't the strength to go on."

"And I'm sad," muttered the Firefly. "For what is life without my wings?"

"Still I do not regret having given up my scales to save you . . ."

"And I am proud to have traded my wings for your freedom . . ."
Then the two lovers fell silent and spoke no more.

In the evening light the lake gave off a passionate glow. Then the light died, and with it died the Goldfish and the Firefly. Whether their souls mingled with the dying light and ascended towards the infinite sky, or dispersed in a cool mist among the flowers, I cannot say. All was quiet, save for the twittering of birds and the humming of honeybees. As for the water lilies, they had closed up their petals and were fast asleep.

IV

The moon rose in the sky, and many fireflies came out to greet it. The wood-elves danced in the moonlight, and the most handsome of them all was the Elf with wings that shone like diamonds.

The Water-Nymph stepped out of her flowerbed and bowed to the moon. On her head she wore a crown of golden scales.

Then she saw the dead bodies of the Firefly and the Goldfish.

"Oh, no!" she shrieked. "Somebody, come quick!" and all the elves stopped dancing and rushed over in a noisy mob.

"What's this?" she exclaimed, pointing at the corpses. "Who has murdered my friends? Who has striped the Firefly of his wings? Who has stripped the Goldfish of her scales?" And she hid her face in her tiny hands and wept.

"They were captured by some children," said the Elf with the wings. "But I freed them in exchange for their best attributes. In fact, I used the Goldfish's scales to fashion the crown that you are now wearing on your head."

"You perfect brute!"

"But did you not say that you wanted the Goldfish's scales? And did I not say that I wanted the Firefly's wings? Tell me, what was I supposed to do if not take them? Surely such things cannot be made by fairy hands alone."

"But you murdered them!" cried the Nymph.

"I did not," replied the Elf. "Those creatures did not need wings or scales to live. Why, I never had wings before, and you never had scales—but we did not die, did we? I tell you, those creatures died on their own accord."

"What a world!" wailed the Nymph. "When I want something, must I take it from another? Must I rob the Goldfish of her scales? Must my gain be another's loss?" And she rushed back to her flower and closed the petals over her.

Then the wood-elves came together and danced a dance of mourning. Only the Elf with the Firefly's wings did not join them. He sat apart on a rock.

"Surely God is a miser," he sighed, staring off into space. "Why, he should have made more firefly wings and goldfish scales. After all, with such a big world to fill, what reason did he have to be so cheap!"

■ ■ ■

Later in the evening the Nobleman's daughter arrived at the lake. She carried a bug-cage in her left hand, and a butterfly net in her right. The Farmer's son arrived soon after. He had a fishbowl in his left hand, and a fishing rod in his right.

"I don't think that I like poor boys," said the girl when she saw him.

"And I don't think that I like rich girls," said the boy.

"Poor boys are always going about in shabby clothes. And what is more, they are cruel."

"Well, clothing is the only clean thing about a rich girl, for their hearts are dirty."

"Last night some awful poor boy murdered my firefly."

"Last night some greedy rich girl murdered my goldfish."

"When I find out which poor boy murdered my firefly, I am going to slap him!"

"And when I find out which rich girl murdered my goldfish, I am going to pull her hair!"

"The next time that I catch something I will put it in the drawing-room window, across from the high garden fence."

"And the next time that I catch something I will put it in the living-room window, behind the old rusty grate."

"I hope that I have not bothered you. Good-bye!"

"Likewise. Good-bye!"

So the two bowed to each other and parted ways, the girl heading off in one direction, the boy heading off in the other.

After the Nobleman's daughter had walked a little way along the lake's edge, she noticed the Wood-Elf sitting alone on a rock.

"Oh," she said to herself; "that must be a Wood-Elf! My nurse has told me all about them." And she stole up to the rock, and tried to grab at Elf; but her foot slipped, and the two of them fell headfirst into the lake.

"Help!" she cried at the top of her voice; and the Wood-Elf, who was just as frightened, called for the King of the Lake, that he might come and save him.

On the other side of the lake, the Farmer's son spied the Water-Nymph sitting pensive in her flower.

"Ah," he said to himself; "that must be a Water-Nymph! My mother has told me all about them." And he stole up to the flower, and tried to grab the Nymph; but he lost his balance, and the two of them fell headfirst into the lake.

"Help!" he cried out; and the Nymph called for the King of the Lake, that he might come and save her.

A moment later the King of the Lake had risen up from the water's deep, and, with a wave of his wand, had rescued the Nobleman's daughter, the Wood-Elf, the Farmer's son, and the Water-Nymph, and set them before him on the shore.

"Who dares disturb this most quiet of places on this most quiet of nights?" he demanded.

"It was the humans!" answered the Wood-Elf.

"Indeed!" nodded the Water-Nymph. "Two good-for-nothing humans!"

"Then you should have drowned them," said the King of the Lake. "Surely you have ways for doing that. Besides, you would be doing the creatures of this lake a favor. Really, you need not have called me out of the deep for this."

As he spoke, one could see that he was seething with rage. "And then there is this business about the Goldfish and the Firefly," he continued. "It is very unbecoming for fairies such as yourselves."

"I wish I had acted differently," admitted the Wood-Elf. "In fact, I spent the whole night reflecting on the matter. But then I got caught by this awful creature here." And he pointed at the Nobleman's daughter.

"I too mourned the loss of our friends," said the Water-Nymph. "But then I got caught by this good-for-nothing creature here." And she pointed at the Farmer's son.

The King of the Lake softened his expression a little.

"Are you the awful creature that tried to catch the Wood-Elf?" he asked, turning to face the Nobleman's daughter.

"I am not an awful creature," said the girl. "I am a Nobleman's daughter, and I like beautiful things. Last night I caught a firefly, but somebody came and stole its wings. Then the firefly disappeared. And tonight, when I saw this little man, I thought that I might catch him and take care of him. But my foot slipped, and I fell into the lake. Oh, you really must believe me. I do not catch beautiful things in order to tease them, but to care for them!"

The King of the Lake smiled and turned to face the Farmer's son.

"And are you the good-for-nothing creature that tried to catch the Water-Nymph?"

"I am not a good-for-nothing creature," said the boy. "I am a Farmer's son, and I like beautiful things also. Last night I caught a goldfish, but somebody came and stole its scales. Then the goldfish disappeared. And tonight, when I saw this little lady, I thought that I might take her home with me—to care for, not to tease!"

The King of the Lake's expression grew softer still.

"And pray," he said, turning to face the Wood-Elf, "why did you treat the Firefly and the Goldfish so cruelly as to strip them of their wings and scales?"

"Because I like beautiful things also," answered the Elf. "And I thought the wings to be exceedingly handsome. And what's more, I wanted to fashion a crown of scales to set upon the Water-Nymph's pretty head. So, yes, I took the wings and scales—but I did not mean to kill the Firefly or the Goldfish!"

"And it is true that I desired the Goldfish's scales," said the Nymph, "and thought the Wood-Elf would look exceedingly handsome with the Firefly's wings. But I never imagined that it would cost the lives of those poor unfortunate creatures!"

At last the King of the Lake revealed a radiant smile.

"I can see that you are all fond of beautiful things. Very well. Many a sin has been forgiven for a love of Beauty. But you must go one step further in your devotion. For it is not right to covet beautiful things. Such a desire comes from a tainted source. A true love of Beauty must spring from a selfless heart. And the greater your love of Beauty, the stronger you will become. That is why men are stronger than beasts; and fairies, stronger than men; and angels, stronger still: because each is more finely attuned to Beauty. Indeed, that is why the one who sees Beauty in all things, and loves all things for the sake of Beauty, is God."

Then the King of the Lake turned to face the Wood-Elf and the Water-Nymph, and said: "Because your love of Beauty was imperfect, you were nearly caught by these children"; and turning to face the children, he said: "Because you coveted beautiful things, you put yourselves in mortal danger. To be sure, a love of Beauty has the power to conquer the universe, but it also has the power to take lives. Remember this, and make no further mistakes"; and—*swoosh, swoosh!*—he waved his magic wand in the air.

V

The Nobleman's daughter awoke to find herself lying on a rock by the shore.

"I don't recall falling asleep here!" she said to herself as she looked round.

Below the Goldfish was swimming about in the calm lake; while above, the Firefly was flickering through the air on his diamond wings.

Then the Farmer's son awoke on the opposite shore.

"I don't recall falling asleep here!" he said to himself as he looked round.

Deep in the forest, the Wood-Elf was dancing a jig in the moonlight; and the Water-Nymph was watching him from her flower and smiling.

The two children's eyes met, and they approached each other.

"I think it's a pity to catch fireflies," said the girl, bowing her head. "Somebody might come along and steal their wings."

"And I think it's a pity to catch fish," replied the boy, bowing his head also. "Somebody might come along and steal their scales."

"I would much rather come here to watch the fireflies."

"And I would much rather come here to watch the goldfish."

So the two of them sat down, side by side, and plucked the flowers wet with dew, and threw them into the water. Handfuls of flowers did the children pluck, and they threw them into the water, one by one.

"Poor boys may go about in dirty rags," said the Nobleman's daughter, "but they are kind. All they need is a fresh pair of clothes and a bath."

"And rich girls may look like Death," said the Farmer's son, "but they have an inner beauty. If only they studied more and exercised outdoors, then the color would return to their faces, and they would grow stronger."

For a few moments there was a brief silence.

"You know," said the Nobleman's daughter, "I am not at all afraid of walking through the woods alone." And her youthful cheeks blushed.

"Well," said the Farmer's son, "I can walk any mountain-path." And his youthful heart quivered.

"I am not afraid of walking mountain-paths. But I would be less lonely if I had someone to walk them with."

"A traveling companion makes the journey more fun."

"Not if they kick at stones or tread on your toes or drag their feet on the ground. I simply cannot stand that."

"Agreed. People should wear clogs and walk at a slow pace. By the by, I think that I will take the high road home."

"I think that I will take it also. I just love to look at the large rocks to the right of it."

"And I like to swing from the big trees to the left of it."

When all the flowers had been plucked, the two children rose to their feet.

"I wouldn't mind it if we walked together, though my nurse might have her concerns."

"And I wouldn't mind it if we walked together, though my friends might tease me."

So they set off through the woods and along the high road.

Meanwhile the Wood-Elf danced in the moonlight, and the Water-Nymph watched him. And the Goldfish and the Firefly, and everybody in and around the lake, dreamed a beautiful spring night's dream.

Chapter Eight

THE MARTYR

THERE ONCE crawled out of a pond a little, tiny Mosquito. He had only just been born. But as soon as his wings had grown large enough, he began to fly about and wonder at all that was around him. And the larger his wings grew, the larger his heart grew also. And the larger his heart grew, the more it filled with Love.

"But where does Love come from," he said to himself as he buzzed about the forest glade, "and with whom shall I share it?"

In the center of the glade there stood a Cow eating grass. On a flower sat a Honey-bee resting her wings. And a Bush Warbler could be heard singing songs from a tree nearby.

The Mosquito trembled all over with joy. "It certainly is a wonderful world!" he sighed and went up to the Honey-bee. "Good morning!" he said. "Why, aren't you lovely? Indeed, you seem to be the loveliest creature in the pond."

"In the pond!" cried the Honey-bee quite angrily. "I am afraid that I know nothing about such dirty, smelly places."

"Oh, dear," said the Mosquito in a timid voice. "I hope that I haven't offended you. But were you really not born in the pond?"

"Certainly not!" snapped the Honey-bee. "To be sure, *you* may have been born in that stink-hole, but *I* was born in an apiary, like a respectable creature, and was raised by a governess." And she raised her pointed stinger in the air.

"That is not a thing to be proud of," snickered the Bush Warbler from his place in the tree. "After all, who isn't raised by a governess these days? Really, you are a person of little importance, whereas I belong to the higher orders, for I was born on a country estate in Java. Of course, it is summer-time there, so I am only here on a sojourn. As to my education, I can assure you that my parents spared absolutely no expense in hiring the finest poets to serve as my teachers. So there is really no comparing us at all."

"Hmph!" snorted the Cow. "What trivial persons you are! Tell me, can either of you say that you were born in an actual house? Well, I can. And what is more, I am told that there were three human beings in attendance for the occasion."

The little Mosquito was quite taken aback. "But regardless of where we are born," he remarked, "surely we can agree that our hearts are one and the same."

"Dear no!" cried the Honey-bee. "For if we are born in different places, then it stands to reason that we ought to have different hearts."

"But I thought that we belonged to a common family," said the Mosquito.

"A common *what*!" cried the Honey-bee. "Why, that would doubtless be an honor for you. But for me, it would be an imposition."

"How so?" asked the Mosquito. "Love is Love, is it not? Surely it is the same for everyone. Take me and the Cow. Though she may be big and I be small, I love her no less than she loves me." And he flew away from the Honey-bee and alighted on the Cow's neck.

"Shoo, fly!" shouted the Cow in an angry manner; and thrashing her ear, she struck the Mosquito hard on his little spindly legs.

The Mosquito fell to the ground.

"Did that hurt much?" said the Cow. "Perhaps it will teach you to know your position, and to keep your opinions to yourself!"

The poor Mosquito winced. The world seemed to him to be a cruel place. "How strange," he murmured as he rubbed his legs. "Here I am thinking that we all belong to a common family, yet nobody will give me the time of day. Indeed, they all act as though I were taking up space. Oh, who could have created such a ridiculous world!"

"It was doubtless created by the old Bee-keeper," said the Honey-bee proudly. "He is very bright and clever, after all."

"The Milkmaid is also clever," said the Cow. "Indeed, she knows just how much hay I require for my diet, and she never forgets to feed my calves either. So I wouldn't be surprised if it were in fact she who created the world."

"Then you must be very ignorant!" laughed the Bush Warbler. "Pray, have neither of you read the Classics? Don't you know that the world was created by God?"

"God?" said the Mosquito, sitting upright and forgetting all about the pain in his legs. "Who is 'God,' and where does he live?"

"According to the poets, he lives in the sky," answered the Bush Warbler.

"Well, you are a poet, are you not?" said the Honey-bee. "Have you seen him?"

But the Bush Warbler shook his head. "I have not," he sighed. "But surely my cousin the Skylark has. He can fly much higher than myself. Ah, here he is now!"

And the Skylark flew down.

"What excellent timing!" said the Honey-bee. "Skylark, I hear that you are quite knowledgeable about the heavens. May I presume, then, that you have met God? Surely he resembles the old Bee-keeper, does he not?"

"You mean to say the Milkmaid," said the Cow.

But the Skylark laughed outright.

"In all my years spent flying about the heavens," he said, "never have I seen anything that so much as resembled a bee-keeper or a milkmaid. I have seen eagles, though, and hawks. Perhaps one of those is God."

"My good cousin," interjected the Bush Warbler, "I fear that you are somewhat mistaken, for eagles and hawks are, like any one of us, merely God's creations. And as everybody knows, God cannot be his own creation."

"Well really!" said a Fly who was passing through the grove. "How arrogant you all sound. I will have you know that I am a research assistant at yonder observatory, where every night I sit on the bald pate of the Chief Astronomer and gaze at the heavens through his mighty telescope, yet never have I confirmed the existence of God. Naturally, I have tried to look for him under the microscope as well, but he was not there. And so I have come to the conclusion that God is simply too small or too distant to be seen. That is to say, his existence is of little importance to our world. Now if you will excuse me, I am on my way to the observatory kitchen, where I intend to engage myself in putting such thoughts to paper."

"I cannot accept your thesis," remarked the Skylark, who was greatly agitated by the Fly's arrogant demeanor. "For while your research is rooted in science, and your argument based on facts, I am inclined to support the theory put forth by the venerable Master Crane, who devoted a considerable effort to exploring the mysteries of God, and who even spent his younger years at the Pyramids studying hieroglyphics. As he explained it to me once when we were flying out to my family estate, the search for God begins not in the observatory or the laboratory, but in a place of worship, such as a temple or a church."

The Skylark then turned his attention to the Mosquito. "As for you, my budding free-thinker, I would advise that you keep a healthy distance from both academia and mythology. Indeed, it would be better for you to search for truth on your own, for discourse and superstition make it exceedingly difficult for one to know anything at all." And flapping his wings, he blew a cloud of dust in the Fly's direction.

"Verily," said the Fly as he dodged the dust and tried to appear open-minded when he was really up against a wall. "Moreover, it is fortunate that there are many temples nearby, and should you wish to begin your fieldwork at once, I would be more than happy to accompany you as a guide—that is, had I not already consented to attend an academic conference at the observatory later today. The conference is to be followed by a banquet, and who else but I am fit to check the food for poison? Indeed, in this great nation of ours, our academics are afforded the utmost respect, and it would be sorely amiss to serve food to such highly esteemed guests without first checking it for poison. Ahem—"; and clearing his throat, he proceeded to recite, word for word, something that he had heard the Chief Astronomer say many times before: "But do not think that we at the observatory are unwilling to accommodate you as you embark upon the commendable path of independent research. Only we regret to inform you that as we are engaged in research of our own, we will be unable to offer you our full support. Nevertheless, we wish you luck with all your scholarly endeavors."

The Mosquito thanked the Fly, and bidding the others farewell, he set off in the direction of the nearest temple.

When he arrived at the temple, he found it to be deserted. "Where is everyone?" he said. "I hope that they haven't all left on vacation."

Then he saw a Sparrow defecating on the statue of a bodhisattva.

"I was told that God lives here," said the Mosquito. "Do you know if he is in?"

"God?" answered the Sparrow. "Do you mean the Buddha? I am afraid that you have missed him. He entered into Nirvana twenty-five thousand years ago, and has not been back since. But perhaps you mean the Christian God. If so, you will have to go to a church to find him."

So the Mosquito flew to the nearest church, where a Congregation happened to be gathered for mass. Large wax candles burned along the white walls and before gilded icons; and every time the Deacon swung the censer, a sweet-smelling incense filled the air. The Priest was dressed in a heavily embroidered gown of golden thread, and together with the Congregation was chanting impassioned pleas to heaven.

The Mosquito alighted on one of the pews and looked round. Everyone had their eyes fixed on the tabernacle. "That must be where God is," he murmured to himself, and stole right up to it and entered in.

And what did he see?

He saw nothing—save for an old blind Spider spinning her web in the dusty air.

The Mosquito gasped and flew out of the tabernacle as fast as his wings could carry him. Outside, the Priest and the Congregation continued their impassioned pleas. Faces that once seemed to express the earnestness of devout prayer now seemed the very picture of madness. Unable to contain himself, the Mosquito cried out: "The tabernacle is empty! There is no God!"

Just then a group of flies who were dancing on one of the stained-glass windows of the church turned round.

"Did you hear that?" exclaimed one. "He says that the tabernacle is empty."

"Well, what did he expect?" said another. "It always has been."

"Dear me!" said a third. "Who is that raving lunatic, after all?"

"Only a young scholar—working on some independent research project, no doubt."

"Well, he won't get anywhere by shouting, will he?"

"Young scholars today are really very immature. Why, they are always trying to pass off common knowledge as their own great discoveries."

The Mosquito let out another cry: "The tabernacle is empty! There is no God!"

But nobody minded. The Congregation and the Priest merely continued their fervent call and response, repeating it again and again.

Suddenly the Mosquito felt as though his whole body were on fire. So desperate was he to make himself heard that at last he leapt onto the Priest's forehead, and screamed: "The tabernacle is empty! There is no God!"

"Damned atheist!" shouted the Priest, and he crushed the Mosquito with his big hand, thus ending the life of the most loving creature there ever was.

■ ■ ■

Some time later, in the barn of the observatory, the Chicken was gossiping with her friends the Duck and the Shepherd Dog.

"Have you heard?" said the Chicken. "The world was created by the old Bee-keeper!"

"I have heard it," answered the Duck. "They say that the Milkmaid helped him."

"Well," said the Chicken, "if what they say is true, then surely the old woman who takes care of us played some part in the matter also."

"And the boy," said the Dog. "We mustn't forget the boy."

"I am not so sure," said the Duck, who always liked to have the last word. "For it is also said that the world was created by God, and so compelling is the argument that many a scholar and benevolent creature has left hearth and home because of it."

"Was there not a little Mosquito who did just that?" whispered a Horse to his neighbor.

"There certainly was," answered a Pig. "And after much study, he concluded that God does not reside within the church. Why, he even told the Priest that his tabernacle was empty, and—*bam!*—that was the end for him."

"Priests are all the same!" cried a big Minorca with a bright red comb on his head. "Best them in an argument and they will have you thrown in jail, or killed even. They are the worst!"

"I know another," said a Cow, and for a while nobody spoke.

"Will God ever be found?" asked a little Chick at last, and the Dog who was desperately trying to scratch at the fleas on his neck, sat upright.

"My dear child," he said gently, "have I not told you the story of my great-great-great grandfather, who served Momotarō on his journey to the Island of the Ogres? Well, it is said that Momotarō brought back from the island a treasure that is known as the Cloak of Invisibility. And if Momotarō could get his hands on a such a wonderous item, I cannot see why God could not do so himself. And if he has, then I am afraid that we are playing a game of hide-and-go-seek that we cannot win. Indeed, God will not be found. That much is clear. And the fact that man is willing to argue otherwise only goes to show how stupid he is."

"Here, here!" cried a voice, and all the creatures in the barnyard cheered.

"Has man always been this way?" said the Chicken to the Duck.

"I am afraid so," she answered. "It is in his genes, after all." And she let out a sigh.

Chapter Nine

THE DEATH OF THE CANARY

I

There once was a wealthy old Housewife who wanted to breed canaries.

"I should like my old hen to have lots of babies this spring," she said to herself one day; and fearing lest her cock should prove ill-equipped for the task, she went out and purchased another younger male. But the three little canaries did not get along well at all and were forever at each other's throats.

"Dear me!" said the Housewife whenever she passed by the cage. "I wonder what is the matter with my canaries? If only they would lay eggs like I asked them to, but all they ever do is fight. And what is worse, I fear that the female is practicing contraception just to spite the males, like those awful suffragettes one hears about. Oh, doesn't she know that it is a dangerous thing, contraception, and must not be practiced without consulting one's doctor?"

But the canaries paid her no heed.

The Female Canary, for her part, could not hold back her feelings. "How awful is woman!" she exclaimed from the topmost perch of the cage. "Why, she fancies that she alone should require makeup and mirrors and veils, and never imagines that we lady canaries might require such things also. Well, I simply won't stand for it, and demand to be given a mirror and makeup, a pair of blue booties, and a photograph of a handsome young actor this instant! We lady canaries are not so old-fashioned, you know."

And looking down at the males, she declared: "Henceforth shall husbands be chosen by general election, to promote the restructuring of the family unit! Is that understood? We lady canaries are more enfranchised than our human counterparts!"

"What!" cried the older Male Canary, raising his head angrily. "Say that again? By general election? How very ridiculous! Why, if that were to be allowed, you senseless females would only ever choose to marry young fools!"

And there was nothing that bothered the older Male Canary more than to see a mature hen fawning over a young cock.

"Just think," he railed on, "were you females to only lay eggs with young males, it would be the downfall of the canary race. A fledging can hardly be expected to raise a respectable bird. Indeed, that is a job for a wise and experienced male. And besides, do you honestly think that we, who are obliged to bear such an immense responsibility in the prime of our lives, would stand idly by while some young chick robbed us of our rightful mates? Balderdash! We are not at all like the cowardly old men of mankind!"

"How rude!" shouted the younger Male Canary, who considered himself a free-thinker and heard in his fat and balding adversary's vociferations an attack upon his treasured idealism. "Have you no manners, or must I beat them into you? Surely the canary race will never be uplifted so long as there are arrogant males like you forcing yourselves on females and spawning idiots wherever you go. Well, I will have you know that unlike the youth of men, we younger male canaries believe in Freedom! Freedom!"

"Freedom, indeed!" responded the older male. "I know well what your 'Freedom' is worth. It is pure seduction! Indeed, you ask that our cage-door be left open when all you really want is to tempt this female to fly away with you!"

"Nothing of the kind!" said the Female Canary timidly. "To be sure, I see nothing wrong with having our cage-door left open, but one can never be too careful, for that capitalist Cat might get in. Oh, he has such long arms and sharp teeth, and is always laying claim to whatever he sees. Really, he is a perfect beast!"

"Silence!" shouted the older male. "I know what your game is! Don't think that I don't."

"Ugh!" said the youth. "You are behaving like a jealous chick! Really, if you are so attached to the idea of sowing seeds, then by all means, go forth and multiply. Give birth to a generation of fools and slobs for all I care. Surely they will be a credit to the race. At any rate, we youths have far more important things to do than to argue with senile old birds."

"I will murder you!" roared the older male, and he lunged at the younger's throat.

"Stop it, you two!" cried the Female Canary, inserting herself between the two males. "Can't you see the need for a general election?"

All of a sudden, the Housewife passed by and saw that the males were fighting again. "Shameless birds!" she exclaimed. "If only you had made babies like I asked you to, you would have lived like kings. But no, all you ever do is fight, and I'm sick of it!" And she gave the cage a good kick.

The cage-door swung open, and a warm spring breeze rushed in.

"Oh, dear!" cried the Female Canary. "Whatever shall we do? Now that capitalist Cat will eat us for sure! Oh, oh!" And she flew to the back of the cage.

In the meantime, the younger Male Canary flew outside and alighted on the veranda.

"I think I should like to see the world," he said softly.

"Then get on with it!" yelled the older male.

"Good-bye!" said the youth, giving one last look to the female.

"Wait for me!" she cried. "Let me come with you!" and she rushed after him.

But the older male blocked her path. "Struggle and I'll wring your neck!" he threatened.

"Oh, let me go!" begged the female, beating her wings in despair. "I want to live! You can't keep me here! I am not a woman. I refuse to be silenced!"

"Well, I am not a man," said her mate. "I refuse to be mocked!"

II

After he had put the battlefield of his cage behind him, the young Canary flew into the garden, where, on the branch of a pink cherry tree, a Sparrow sat lecturing a school of fledglings. The Sparrow was a wise professor who had often stopped by the canary cage to extoll the virtues of socialism to the captive birds inside.

The Canary was thrilled to see such a distinguished bird. "Professor!" he chirruped as he alighted on the branch next to him. "It certainly has been a while! As you can see, I am free at last and ready to learn how best to further the socialist cause."

"Socialist!" exclaimed the Sparrow, looking sharply at the youth. "No, I am afraid you have me mistaken for someone else."

But the Canary was an honest bird; and as such, he failed to understand the danger of speaking one's politics in public.

"But Professor," he said, "you used to come to our cage to talk socialism, did you not?"

"I did no such thing!" cried the Sparrow. "What on earth makes you think that?"

"I distinctly recall you saying that one day all the world would march together towards a bright socialist future, and that this was an indisputable fact."

"Ridiculous!" said the Sparrow, and he looked round him nervously. "You fool!" he went on in a low voice. "Don't you know that it is dangerous to speak in terms of facts? Why, there is a difference between what one says in one's cage and what one says in the world. After all, in the world, there is nothing more variable than a fact. Indeed, facts change all the time. Which way will the wind blow? What will the weather be? Where stands the sun and the moon? One must observe facts in all their variations. Indeed, an understanding of their mutability is paramount to one's success in the world. And those lacking such a faculty must simply step aside. Now, if we were more like man, who is infinitely superior to us, we might build jails and asylums, to which we could ship off our undesirables as fast as possible. But I digress . . . You say that you want to be a socialist? Pooh! That is nothing to be proud of. Better a parrot than a socialist crow—that's what I say. At least you would entertain the masses. Meanwhile, those socialist crows are shunned as harbingers of doom wherever they go, and no one dares to so much as look at them. Oh, how I wish I could talk with you a little while longer, but I am expected to deliver a speech on communism in which I have been asked to sing the praises of some autocratic state. Ah, but such is the life of a poor professor!"

III

Some time later, in a small grove at the edge of town, a meeting was underway. It had been organized by a gang of socialist crows. Sentinels were posted to the trees in every direction, while seated on the topmost bough of a great pine tree, the Chair-Crow was delivering a fiery speech on the state of socialism.

"They call us radicals," he declared. "We are feared everywhere and welcomed nowhere. There is no end to the indignities that we face from every creature. But tell me, are we deserving of such treatment? And is the paradise for which we strive so terrible?"

There was a pause for effect, during which he surveyed the crows that filled the upper and lower galleries of the neighboring trees.

"Incoming officer!" shouted one of the Sentries.

"What!" cried the Chair-Crow. "Has nobody paid our respects to the police?" And he glared at his Secretary with the crazed eyes of a despot.

"But sir, the meeting has just begun. It's too early to pay our respects."

"Nonsense!" thundered the indignant Chair-Crow. "Don't you know that we must pay our respects to the police both before *and* after each meeting? Oh, if only our police were more like that of man! Surely *they* don't take bribes! In any event, go and see who it is that is coming. And if he looks strong, you are to be courteous and allow him passage. But if he looks weak, you are to bring him to me at once."

A few minutes later the Sentry returned with the young Canary.

"Now," said the Chair-Crow in a lordly voice, "what is your reason for coming here?"

"I am but a simple youth looking for answers to the problems confronting our society," said the Canary in all seriousness. "And hearing that you crows are the most ardent of socialists, I thought that I might carry out my research as a member of your party."

"That is all well and good," said the Chair-Crow, "but what do you intend to do about that colorful coat of yours?"

"My coat?" said the Canary, looking over his plumage. "Will I be obliged to don a black robe for the duration of my studies?"

"Naturally," answered the Chair-Crow. "And though you may have heard that human socialists are fond of dressing up in silk shirts, frock coats, and shiny black shoes; that they drink warm sake, cold beer, and fine wines—or whatever it is their friend is drinking, so long as they don't have to pay for it themselves; and that they frequent restaurants, theaters, and brothels so as to better understand the plight of the proletariat, we are of a different mind, finding it proper to wear the same clothes, eat the same food, and have the same standard of living as each other. Pray, what are your thoughts on eating rotten meat?"

"I cannot say that I would like to," said the Canary apologetically.

"What about regular meat?"

"The same."

"What do you eat, then?"

"Chestnuts and barnyard grass."

"What luxury!" snorted the Chair-Crow in a disgusted manner. "Then you are no doubt the pet of some capitalist pig. What are your thoughts on theft and deceit? To be sure, this is more in line with the skills of human socialists, but do you think that you could manage it?"

"I am afraid not."

"So you are not even cut out to be a human socialist! Some nerve you have wanting to join our party. What can you offer us?"

"I can sing!"

"A poet!" exclaimed the Chair-Crow. "So you are an aspiring nightingale? Well then, would you care to sing us one of your songs?"

The little Canary was so naïve that he completely failed to hear the condescension in the Chair-Crow's words; and shaking out his golden feathers, which glittered in the light of the sun, he began to sing, and his voice was like a silver bell.

> I see flowers bloom
> And my soul yearns for freedom
> I smell their perfume
> And my heart leaps with joy
> I listen to the brook
> Thread its way through the grove
> While I wait for the advent
> Of our happy freedom
> Like small waves washing
> The shores of our hardship—
> Knowing in my heart
> That one day it will come

Then, when he had finished his song, the crows all burst out laughing.

"Hah!" snickered the Chair-Crow. "Do you honestly think that by singing such a ridiculous song you are qualified to join our hallowed ranks? And do you expect us to go out of our way to find you chestnuts and barnyard grass? No, we are not so kind. We are not artists or priests. We are not at all like those stupid human beings who keep useless creatures for pets."

The Canary felt the eyes of all the crows upon his plumage.

"So if you really are intent on joining us," continued the Chair-Crow, "you can start by removing that radiant coat of yours." And turning to his fellow crows, he issued a terrifying order: "Come, let us help the poet with his coat!"

At this, a swam of crows fell upon the Canary, laughing and jeering as they pulled out his feathers, one by one. Unable to fight back, let alone cry, the young Canary simply allowed the crows to have their way with him.

Before long, a Sentry signaled the arrival of a hunter, and, in an instant, the crows all flew away. For a time the grove resounded with the flurry of beating wings, but this gradually subsided, replaced by the sound of rustling leaves.

"Oh, dear!" exclaimed a timid gray Squirrel as she cautiously put her head out of her hole. "Those socialists can be so cruel."

"Why does one need to wear black to be a socialist anyways?" said a little Field-Mouse from her nest. "I do not find their robes to be particularly attractive! They are certainly not as pretty as what the Canary was wearing."

"Indeed," said the Squirrel. "And if it really was necessary for him to wear black, could they not have doused him with ink? Why, they tore off all of his feathers, the poor thing! How it must have pained him."

Droplets of blood trickled from the body of the Canary. With his forehead pressed against the foot of a tree, he stared into a pool of his own blood and began to weep. Then, in a voice filled with pain and sadness, he sang—

I have purchased my freedom
With these blood-red rubies . . .

But before he could sing any more, a fat black Cat crawled out from under a bush. "Who is that I hear singing?" he said, licking his lips. "Why, if it isn't the Canary who escaped from my master's home. All right, back to your cage! Don't make me hurt you!"

The Canary did not have the strength to stand. His body was battered and bruised, and his heart was broken beyond repair.

"I am an artist who longs for freedom," whispered the Canary weakly. "I cannot go back to singing in a cage."

"Silence!" hissed the Cat. "Haven't you learned your lesson? Why, if it weren't for us capitalists, you artists would never survive." And he extended his claws to their full extent.

"I would rather starve than die by your claws!" cried the Canary, and he tried to fly away.

"Foolish bird!" growled the Cat, pinning the Canary down with his claws. "A little taste of freedom has given you dangerous thoughts. Ah, this is why I always say that canaries and nightingales should be locked up in cages. Now allow me teach you a lesson!" And he stripped the Canary from head to tail.

When he had finished, the Cat licked his paws and washed his face. "One must be tough with these artistic types," he muttered under his breath, "or else they will never learn." And he went his own way home.

The Squirrel reappeared at her hole, shivering with fear.

"How frightening!" she said, "I can still feel my heart racing. This is the first time I have seen a bird murdered in cold blood."

"Me too," said the Field-Mouse from her nest. "Pray, is that what they call a capitalist?"

"Yes, that was the capitalist Cat. He is said to keep a Housewife as his pet, and he always uses brute force to get what he wants."

"He is too cruel."

"Too cruel."

"But you know," added the Field-Mouse. "As cruel as that capitalist Cat is, he only ever strips the skin from his prey once, whereas human capitalists are not even satisfied after they have stripped the skin of a laborer ten times or more. Human beings are backwards creatures; but the cruelty of their capitalists is really something else."

"Socialist, capitalist," sighed the Squirrel, "what is the difference—they are all enemies of us honest creatures, are they not?"

"For sure," nodded the Field-Mouse. "But especially the capitalists . . ."

IV

The next day the old Housewife was sitting in her bedroom watching her young Maid as she dusted the furniture.

"Madam," said the Maid, "I hear that the young canary that escaped from its cage yesterday met a terrible end. First it was scolded by a sparrow, then it got bullied by some crows, and finally it was eaten by the cat."

"Oh, that is too sad," said the Housewife. "But you know, after it left, the other canaries calmed right down. No doubt it is with birds as it is with people. Say all that you want about free love and restructuring the family unit, there is nothing better than monogamy."

"Especially when the woman is younger," said the Maid.

"Youth has nothing to do with it," remarked the Housewife. "For grace and wisdom are what really matter." And catching a glimpse of the Maid's slender neck, she added: "But you should have a young man yourself. You are a young woman after all."

"I wouldn't mind an older man," sighed the Maid. "Someone like your husband perhaps. Older men can be so kind, wouldn't you say?"

"Get out!" screamed the Housewife at the very top of her voice. "And tell my husband to come and see me this instant. Ugh! Men—why, they are all the same! Incapable of distinguishing between a lady and a common housemaid. Ah, but that is the democratic spirit for you!" And she slammed the bedroom door shut.

Chapter Ten

THE MAD CAT

I WISH that I could forget that day. I really do. But I can't.

It was the last day of the year. The streets were empty and cold. Colder still was my heart, much colder; and much more empty, my soul—not that there exists an instrument for measuring such things.

I sat by the stove and stared into space, lost in thought. What naïve hopes and dreams I still carried in my heart burned faintly there among the embers. All of a sudden, Tora came scampering into the room. Tora is the family cat. He dove straight into my lap and clung to me by all fours, shaking. What could be the matter, I wondered.

"Young master," he said in a whisper, "you are the only one who loves me, the only one who cares . . ."

"Ugh!" I thought to myself. "Not another dream! I am sick of dreams! But then I am even more sick of reality."

I sat motionless and silent.

Tora started up again. "Young master," he said, "I can't go on. I have lost all hope."

"*Oh, shush! I myself lost hope long ago, but you don't see me complaining!*" is how I would have answered had I not pitied the poor creature. So I said nothing.

Tora went on. "They all call me lazy—your father, the maid, the cook. And for what? Because I have stopped catching mice! But I am not lazy, I tell you. I simply refuse to hunt. I no longer have it in me. Just look at my teeth, my claws—are they not still sharp? Ah! But you see, the problem is here," he said, tapping his breast, "in my heart. For deep down, I have lost the will to hunt. And now the mice have gotten into the pantry and are eating their way through the rice. They are biting holes through the bread and are pilfering the sweets. In fact, just the other day, I heard your mother complaining that they had nibbled the pages of her favorite book—What was it again? Ah yes, Kroptkin's *The Conquest of Bread*! 'Oh, those naughty little mice!' they all say. But they are not naughty—they are starving! Literally starving. And if they can't eat, they must die. Oh, young master, you must believe me. Look into my eyes!"

Tora had worked himself into a frenzy, and dug his sharp claws into my thighs that I might take him more seriously.

"*Ouch! You stupid cat. Don't get smart with me! I can't believe you are getting worked up over a couple of starving mice. Look at Russia or Germany or Austria, for that matter—a hundred million people are starving there, maybe more. But do you see us humans raising the alarm? Really, I hope those disease-infested rodents starve to death; so much the better!*" is how I would have answered had I the strength to do so.

Tora went on: "Because I refuse to hunt, your father has ordered that I not be fed. But you knew that, didn't you? Well, let me tell you, I am starving now, and I cannot stand it; the pain is near unbearable. And if I try to take something for myself, they will call me a thief and begin to shout. But my stomach grumbles, young master, and I am too famished to steal. Oh, I can't go on! They all think that not feeding me will make me want to hunt again. But it won't work, I tell you. For deep down, a part of me is gone—the killer's instinct. Oh, I can't go on! So I must be mad—yes, if I were human, that is what they would call me—mad!"

"*Yes, perhaps they would. But behind your back they are more likely to call you a 'moron' or an 'idiot' or worse,*" is what I would have said had I the strength to do so.

Tora went on: "You see, it all started one day when I was in the pantry, waiting for the mice to show up. I knew it was the rice that they wanted. And indeed, when they arrived, they were all chanting, 'Rice! Rice! Give us the rice!' over and over. There was, as it were, a sea of them. So I went to work. I must have killed a hundred, a thousand, ten thousand—who knows, really? But the more I killed, the hungrier I became. There were big mice, little mice, black mice, grey mice, males, females, parents, children! All chanting wildly, as if their words were scripture. 'Rice! Rice! Give us the rice,' they shouted with each new wave. Oh, there seemed to be no end to them. It was as if an infinite number of mice—from the dawn of time to the end of days—were rushing upon me all at once. And with each new wave, their chanting became more terrible, more tenacious: 'Rice! Rice! Give us the rice!' they cried again and again. All of a sudden, I began to feel strange. At first I thought that I was hearing the cries of mice, but among them I heard something more familiar—the cries of cats! Louder and louder they grew, till they drowned out the mice, and all that I could hear were the ear-splitting cries of my brothers and sisters. 'Rice! Rice! Give us the rice!' Indeed, there was no mistaking it. What I heard in those cries were cats. I was afraid. I lost control. I ran. For a long time, I sat shivering in a dark corner, the cry of 'Rice! Rice! Give us the rice!' resounding in my ears, interminably. My hairs bristled for hours, days, months, it seemed. That is when I knew I could not go on, for I had gone mad. That is when I began to see that the mice were in fact my brothers and sisters, that they too deserved love and compassion! That is when I lost the will to hunt. And so I was forced to steal. And do you know what? Then it all made sense—how the mice are my true brothers and sisters. Well, now my friends all call me mad, even those nearest and dearest to me. 'You are a mad cat!' they cry and run away. I have been found out. Everybody in the house knows my secret. So yesterday your father ordered that I be hanged. But I do not want to be hanged! That is why I need you, young master. I need you to buy me morphine. I need you to put me to sleep. I need you to take pity on me!"

Tora had spoken for a long time; and to make sure that I was still listening, he dug his sharp claws into my thighs once more.

"Ouch!" I cried. "That hurt!"

I returned to my senses. In my lap I saw Tora, clinging to me by all fours, shivering. I stroked his back gently, still somewhat dazed. The fire from the stove had gone out, and with it my hopes and dreams.

My father crept into the room. Like a thief he stole up behind me, and thrusting out a bag, he pulled it over Tora's head.

"Ah-ha!" he shouted. "I got him! I got the little beast!"

I started and nearly fell over.

"Father!" I cried, catching my breath. "What—what's gotten into you?"

"This little beast is mad. Mad I tell you! Just be thankful that he didn't scratch you. I just spoke to the animal doctor. He says I should kill him now, before he ends up hurting one of us."

"And you're going to do it?"

"Of course," he said, as if no explanation were necessary. "I meant to do it yesterday, but he got away, the sly devil." And he went towards the door.

I could hear Tora crying, writhing, trying to get out of the bag. But his voice was oddly weak and empty. It was the loneliest voice in the world.

I got up and ran to the door.

"Wait!" I cried, grabbing hold of the bag my father carried in his hands.

"What do you want?"

"Don't you feel sorry for it?"

"Sorry for what? It's a mad cat."

"Don't say that, Father. Please, I'm begging you. Let him go."

"Fool!"

"At least, don't beat him to death, please. Let *me* kill him. Let me go and buy him some morphine. Let me put him to sleep."

He stared at me.

"What a sentimental little brat you are! I have never heard of anything so stupid."

"But Father, please . . ."

"Shut up!" he shouted and struck me square in the jaw.

Then he left the room.

I began to feel strange.

"Young master!"

It was Tora. But this time I wasn't dreaming. I could actually hear him.

"Please, you must save me! Save me!"

Soon his voice was joined by the voices of other cats and mice, and together they formed a ghastly chorus.

"Young master, we are starving; they are killing us!

"Young master, please, you must save us!"

The cries echoed. I tried to cover my ears, but it was to no use. They echoed through my body, till the very tips of my fingers were tingling, such was their strength. Then the number of voices multiplied and grew louder. They were strengthened by an infinite family of cats and mice—stretching from the dawn of time to the end of days. I no longer understood what was happening. I understood nothing at all. There was but one thought—one thought that came to me from the black and swirling abyss of my world—

"I can't go on!"

It came to me so clearly, as if it had been carved in white relief.

"Rice! Rice! Give us the rice!"

"Young master, please, save us! We are starving, they are going to kill us! Young master, please save us!"

"Help!" I cried, half in a daze. "Somebody! Anybody!"

A servant girl appeared at the doorway.

"Is the young master alright?"

"Come here," I murmured.

The servant girl took a few steps into the room. She looked concerned.

"Does the young master need something?"

"Closer, closer . . ."

"Tell me, young master, what is it you need?"

I put my lips to her ear and whispered: "I want you to fetch me some morphine."

The servant girl stepped back in shock.

"And what—what might the young master want the morphine for?"

"I can't go on. I'm a moron, an idiot, mad."

The servant girl's face turned white as a sheet.

"What on earth are you saying?"

"You see, I had this thought: that we all might be brothers and sisters—the cats, the mice, the servants of the house, all of us. In fact, it is not merely a thought, but a conviction. I feel it strongly, here, in my heart. We all deserve love and compassion. We are all brothers and sisters . . ."

My voice trembled.

The servant girl stared at me, silent, tears shining in her eyes.

I wish that I could forget that day. I really do. But I can't. I can't . . .

Chapter Eleven

FOR THE SAKE OF MANKIND

INTRODUCTION

My father is a somewhat recognized biologist, though not famous by any means. Most of his friends are biologists like himself. And while some of them conduct all sorts of experiments on living animals, others, like my father, do not. But then there are still others who run big hospitals where I hear that they torture their most vulnerable human patients for the sake of scientific research. In any event, this is all to say that I sometimes hear strange stories—the story that I am about to tell to you being one of them.

I

In a certain city there lived an eminent biologist by the name of K, whose research into the human nervous system was celebrated at home and abroad.

Now this K was said to keep hundreds of rabbits, rats, and dogs for experimental purposes. And though his laboratory was set quite far back from the street, passers-by would sometimes hear the blood-curdling cries of animals emanating from inside—cries that almost sounded like desperate pleas to the human heart.

"Not another experiment!" some gasped whenever they heard the cries, and hurried on their way as fast as their legs could carry them.

However, others who lived in the neighborhood were so used to the noises that came out of K's laboratory that they hardly noticed them at all.

Only K's nine-year-old son could not get used to the cries. And whenever they became too much for him, he would leap out of doors like a madman—hands over his ears, eyes closed, mind blank—and run for miles.

This made K very upset. "What a moron! What a degenerate!" he would yell; and waving his hands fiercely in front of his face, as if to block out some terrible thought, would hole himself up in his laboratory for two or three days. On such occasions, the distressed cries that emanated from his laboratory were the worst.

Such behavior led everyone to believe that K had a terrible temper.

One day, when K was in a particularly bad mood, there came from the laboratory a gut-wrenching howl of pain.

When she heard it, K's wife sat down with her son and held him tight, lest he should run. The poor boy covered his ears to block out the noise.

Then there came a different cry, the piercing yelp of a dog.

The boy turned pale. "Mother!" he cried out. "That's L! I know it! That's L!" And he broke free of his mother's hold.

Of all the animals in K's house, the little dog L was by far the smartest and most talented, and K's son loved him dearly.

K's son ran into the laboratory, and leaping onto the dissection table, tried to grab a hold of his father's scalpel.

But before him loomed two wide, unmoving eyes; a hard, frightful face; and trembling lips over which bubbled surf-like foam.

"Moron! Idiot! Degenerate!" roared K, brandishing his large scalpel threateningly.

"Stop! Stop!" cried K's wife as she rushed into the room.

But she was too late. Unable to stop the downward thrust of her husband's hand, she watched the scalpel enter her child's skull.

The boy gasped, and throwing his hands over his blood-soaked head, toppled over beside his faithful dog on the dissection table.

With uncomprehending eyes, K's wife stared at her collapsed son, then at her husband, and then at the bloody scalpel in his hand.

"What have you done?" she said, barely sounding the words.

Meanwhile, K wondered at the fresh blood dripping from the scalpel. "Moron . . . Idiot . . . Degenerate," he muttered mechanically.

Both boy and dog lay perfectly still.

II

K treated his son's wound, and in three months' time, the boy made a near-full recovery. Only a wide scar extending from his forehead to the back of his skull remained. Whether this scar on his head, or the scar on his heart, ever fully healed, I cannot say.

Little L survived also, and went yapping cheerfully about the house as he had done before the laboratory incident—though I cannot say that the scar on his heart fully healed either.

At any rate, as soon as his son had recovered, K threw himself back into his work with twice the vigor, so as to make up for lost time. And after a silence of three months, the distressed cries of animals returned with a greater intensity.

Indeed, the biologist's mood seemed to be worsening with each passing day. Even his closest friends trembled to look at his dark face and lifeless eyes.

"No matter how many years and how many animal lives we waste," he said to a party of guests one night after diner, "all of our labor only ever amounts to a kind of hypothesis. But I know a way by which we can obtain better results within weeks . . ."

His guests eyed him doubtfully.

"To do this," K went on, a black light flashing in his eyes, "we cannot use rabbits or dogs. Instead, we must use human beings . . ."

"Please, dear," his wife murmured, "that's enough."

But K was not listening.

"And so," he continued in a low voice, "if you would permit me to use one, but *one* human being—a degenerate even—I believe that I would be able to complete my study of the human nervous system in a matter of weeks. Ah, just think of how my research would benefit not only the nation, but all mankind! And all that I am asking for is one human being, one single degenerate, for the sake of mankind . . ."

As his strangely gleaming eyes surveyed the room, they stopped upon his son, who was sitting quietly in a corner.

"Mother!" cried the boy when he felt the heat of his father's stare upon him, and his mother wrapped her arms around him, to shield him from her husband's sight.

The guests all stared at K in shock.

"I said, that's enough, dear!" exclaimed K's wife.

From outside the house there came the lonely howl of L. It seemed to echo down, way down, to the very depths of the soul.

■ ■ ■

That night in bed, K's son called for his mother, and when she arrived, he hugged her tight and whispered into her ear.

"Tell Father that I will do anything for the sake of mankind. I will be like a dog for him . . . for the sake of mankind . . ."

I cannot put into words how sorry the boy's mother must have felt to hear her son speak this way, nor shall I endeavor to try.

Holding her child in her arms, she sobbed.

"Oh, my poor baby!"

From out of the dark night, there came the lonely howl of L. It seemed to echo down, way down, to the very depths of the soul.

III

It was a dark night. And no matter how hard he tried, the boy could not get to sleep. So when the house had become perfectly quiet, he slipped out of bed and went outside.

"L! L!" he called out.

"Young master!" answered L, flying out of the darkness like a ghost. "You've come!"

"What, is this a dream?" wondered the boy, rubbing his eyes. "But it must be; otherwise you would not be talking to me."

"Come along to my house," said L. "There is a matter that we must discuss"; and he guided the boy through the warm night by the hem of his nightgown.

"But how is it that you can talk? Dogs can't talk!"

"Why not? Surely there is no harm in it."

"I suppose you are right. But such logic only holds true in dreams."

They came to a little dog house, the entrance to which, strange to say, was large enough for the boy to enter into without any trouble.

Inside, the boy saw a woman who looked remarkably like his mother, and a young boy who looked remarkably like his older cousin.

"Good evening, Mother!" announced L as he entered. "You will notice that I have brought with me the young master."

The woman bowed. "Welcome," she said in a friendly voice.

"Pardon me," said K's son, bowing in turn, and looking slightly embarrassed. "I hope that you will forgive me for intruding in my nightgown."

Then he noticed that L was on his hind-legs and removing his dog-skin like a boy removes his uniform after coming home from school.

A moment later there stood before him a sweet little boy of his own age.

"What a trick!" exclaimed K's son. "You certainly had us fooled!"

"Allow me to introduce you to my mother," said L, smiling.

The woman bowed again. "Hello, dearie. My name is H. Thank you for taking care of my son. He assures me that you are a very good boy."

K's son wanted to say, "You're welcome," but he felt something choking him in his throat.

"The bones and bread you fed us for breakfast were very delicious, I might add."

K's son wanted to say, "It was nothing," but, again, he could not, so he bowed his head slightly in acknowledgment.

"This here is S," said L, gesturing to the handsome sixteen-year-old. "We *might* be related—that is, if his father is indeed one of your father's bulldogs. However, if his father is one of those bulldogs owned by the rich man across the street, it is a different story."

S greeted K's son as a senior middle school student might greet a junior middle school student—that is, with a simple nod.

K's son bowed his head in acknowledgment.

Suddenly he felt a wet kiss on his cheek.

It was L. "Shall we wrestle?" the dog-boy asked enthusiastically. "I won't go easy this time, I promise"; and the two began to grapple as they normally would on the lawn.

Playing the part of referee, S ran about, yelling, "All right! All right! Let's see some spirit now, boys! All right! All right!"

After they had finished wrestling, L's mother gave K's son a fish head, and L a fish tail. K's son politely refused his portion and offered it to S.

All this time, he could not stop looking at the dog-skin that L had removed earlier. So when an opportunity availed itself, he picked it up and studied it closely.

"What is the matter?" asked S. "Didn't you know the insides of dogs and cows and birds and fish are exactly like that of man? The only difference is the clothes we wear!" and he laughed like an adult might laugh at a child.

Oh, shut up, thought K's son. *I'm not stupid.*

"You see," L added, "tens of thousands of years ago, our ancestors used to wear the same clothing as fish. Then we switched to canine clothing. Who knows, perhaps ten thousand years from now, we'll be proudly walking about in suits and dresses, like man!"

"I believe they call it 'evolution,'" murmured L's mother hesitantly.

"Only don't think that humans are necessarily more evolved than anyone else. Certainly, a large number of them are degenerates."

K's son blushed in embarrassment. How he hated *that word*! They must have heard his father use it, he thought to himself.

"Doubtless, most human beings are good for nothing," sighed S. "They should really try living in our skin before claiming to be evolved." And he eyed K's son.

"Don't mind him," interjected L's mother, looking worriedly at the boy's flushed face. "He's not referring to you or your father . . ."

K's son said nothing. Then, after a pause, he began to put on L's dog-skin.

"Oh! Oh!" yapped L. "How fun!"

Then, when K's son had finished dressing, everybody clapped their hands, and exclaimed: "Good doggie! Good doggie!"

IV

K's son was in his room, the walls of which were awash with morning light. The warm rays of the sun danced across his sleepy face.

"Ugh," groaned the boy, "it's so hot!" and he opened his eyes. "What a stupid dream," he continued softly to himself. "Why do humans have such stupid dreams? To think that I dreamed I was wearing L's skin . . ." And he glanced at the mirror on the wall in front of him and started at the adorable little dog staring back at him.

"No, it can't be!" cried the boy. "I'm a dog? Oh, Mother, come quick! I'm a dog! I'm L! I've degenerated! Oh, Mother, come quick!"

When his mother, who was preparing his father's breakfast, heard the commotion, she rushed over and saw her son crawling round his room on all fours, yapping and growling and making all kinds of bizarre sounds.

"My baby!" she exclaimed. "What's wrong?"

Her son bounded over to her and began licking her hand. He did not speak—he only barked gleefully a great many times.

"What's going on in there?" shouted K from the dining room.

"Nothing!" answered his wife as she locked the door. "Nothing at all. You just stay where you are." And getting down on her knees, she hugged her child tight, and kissed him in the hope that it would quiet his frightful yapping.

The bright morning sun danced joyfully on all the walls of the room.

K appeared at the window. Casting a look of disdain on his family, he turned round and stormed off towards his laboratory.

Not long after that, there could be heard the most crazed howls of pain and suffering, which strangely harmonized with the boy's yapping.

"My baby!" wailed the mother while the bright rays of the morning sun stepped lightly across the walls to the disturbing choir of voices.

■ ■ ■

That night, when all was quiet, the mother tried to tuck her darling child into bed, but he slipped through her hands and bounded outside, running through the darkness till he came to the little dog house, where L and the others were waiting for him.

"Young master!" they exclaimed when he came in. "Take off that dog skin quickly! We all heard the commotion today."

"It was awful!" answered K's son, undressing. "No one would listen to me. Really, I am quite beside myself with sadness."

"Of course you are," said L's mother. "And how worried your mother must have been. Now, hurry on home." And she ushered him to the entrance of the dog house.

"Please visit us again," said L eagerly. "Mother says that she is sewing you your very own dog-skin, so that we can both play together as dogs!"

So K's son returned to his room, where his exhausted mother lay sleeping in her nightgown. In the low lamplight, he was struck once again by her uncanny resemblance to H. Only her eyes were more red with tears, and her cheeks more pale with worry.

He stood silent for a time, watching her. Then, placing his hand upon her shoulder, he shook her lightly.

"Mother?" he said softly. "Mother, wake up. I'm a little boy again. See? I'm not a degenerate. I'm a little boy again."

His mother awoke with a start.

"Mother," the child went on, "you see, the difference between a man and a dog is only skin deep. We are exactly the same inside. L and I are no different from each other. And the same can be said about H and you."

His mother smiled, and her beautiful eyes filled with tears.

V

K's research was progressing steadily. And the more it progressed, the longer his eyes would linger on L's head. That head, those intelligent, human-like eyes, seemed to be more precious than those of any other creature in the house.

Then one day both L and K's son disappeared, and nobody—not the neighbors nor the police—could say where they had gone.

What was more, K had locked the door to his laboratory to ensure that he would not be disturbed.

After three days, K's wife was finally admitted into the lab.

"They still haven't found him . . ." she said mournfully.

But K made her no answer.

"They haven't found L either," she continued. "What do you think happened to them?"

Without speaking a word, K pointed to a full body of animal fur hanging on the wall.

His wife went over and placed her hand on it. After a moment of study, she pointed to the head, on which there could be seen a wide scar, made by a scalpel, stretching from the forehead to the back of the skull.

"It's L!" she exclaimed. "But L never had such a scar on his head, did he?"

K's lips trembled. "You're raving . . . You're mad . . ." he murmured.

"You would like that wouldn't you?" his wife said coldly. "Then you could dissect me for your research . . . For the sake of mankind!"

■ ■ ■

K's wife was never seen again.

The neighborhood was deeply saddened. K's friends and colleagues chose to believe that the mother and child had gone to live with relatives in another city. Meanwhile, the domestic workers in the neighborhood all whispered about how terrible cries of pain had been heard coming from K's laboratory on the days each had disappeared.

But the rumors died down eventually. For a short two weeks after the unfortunate incident, K published a paper on the human nervous system, and the findings were hailed at home and abroad as a revolution in modern science . . .

Some time after that, K was bitten by one of his dogs and died.

On his desk he left the following letter:

To the person who finds my body,

I have just been bitten by a mad dog. A small mad dog . . .
It snuck into my lab when I wasn't looking.

Why?

Those unmoving eyes, that gaping mouth, that drooling
tongue—I knew straight away that it was mad. So taking
up my scalpel, I prepared myself to strike it dead. And yet,
even after having dissected thousands of living creatures,
I found myself lacking the strength to kill this one small
mad dog.

I could have run. But I didn't.

Why?

I cannot say. I am not a doctor of emotions. I am only a
biologist . . .

The second after that small dog bit me, it jumped into
my lap and began licking my hand. I have never expressed
warmth to another creature, I have never even kissed my own
child before, and yet this little dog kept licking my hand again
and again.

Why?

This may sound odd, but at that moment, for the first time in
my life I wanted to write poetry; I wanted to perform Chopin's
Nocturnes or Grieg's Spring lyric. I wondered then why I had
never told my child beautiful fairy tales.

We all have our regrets . . .

So without further ado, I will chloroform myself and die
singing Ave Maria . . .

K

The biggest mystery to K's friends was that the small dog discovered with his corpse was none other than the missing L . . .

VI

A few years ago, I went to visit a colleague of my father who had looked after me when I was in university. The hospital he helped to establish, and its laboratory, are still widely regarded as second to none.

The doctor had just finished conducting a very significant experiment when I called on him at his laboratory.

Sitting down on the couch in his lab, I took a long look at his face, which I had always known to be thin and pale. Today it appeared flushed, and unusually full of life.

As he specialized in the human nervous system, our conversation naturally turned to talk of K and his contributions to the field.

"I could never commit myself to my work as thoroughly as he did," admitted the doctor frankly. "He was so detail-oriented. A man in pursuit of truth. Ah, but that is why his research will likely not be improved upon for some two, three hundred years. What a genius he was! That is for certain. However, in looking closely at his research, one can clearly see how his methods differ from those of other scientists."

"His methods?"

"Indeed."

I stared at him doubtfully. "You mean, how he used rats and rabbits and dogs?"

The doctor chucked enigmatically. "I mean," he said in a low voice, "that he experimented on at least two human beings. Surely you have heard about his wife and child?"

"Yes," I nodded. "My father told me that they disappeared."

"They weren't the only ones . . ."

I was thunderstruck.

"My dear boy," the doctor went on, his fingers playing with a scalpel on his desk, "in today's society, no one bats an eye when ambitious politicians and military generals slaughter tens of thousands of young persons for land or commerce. And yet we deem it reprehensible for a man of science to experiment on one human life—even if it be the life of a degenerate—for the sake of mankind and human happiness. Such is our modern humanitarianism, the twentieth-century civilization we pride ourselves on!"

He walked over to the door and locked it.

"Even our 'model citizens' think nothing of committing crimes against the most vulnerable members of society. But a man of science cannot kill one senseless idiot to progress his research, for the sake of world happiness? Ha! Such is the morality of civilized man!"

The doctor's dark eyes were flashing madly, and the scalpel in his hands flickered ominously before me.

There was nowhere to run—not that I thought to run at the time. On the contrary, I instinctively threw my hands over my head.

"Just do it already!" I shouted. "For the sake of mankind!"

The doctor's face softened, and he again appeared to me as the kind old man from my university days.

He put the scalpel down.

"I was only joking," he said, putting his hand on my shoulder. "You knew that, right?"

"Of course . . ."

The doctor unlocked the door, and I got up to say good-bye.

"But," I said, giving him a firm handshake, "*I* wasn't joking. If you ever need me . . . for the sake of mankind, just let me know. It'll be our little secret. I don't care. I'll be like that dog, L. Only don't let anybody know . . ."

■ ■ ■

I returned home and went straight to my father's laboratory.

"What really happened to K's wife and child?"

My father started and looked at me.

"His wife and child?" he said. "Why, they disappeared."

"Is that all?"

"All that is known."

"But I heard K experimented on at least two human beings. His research suggests so."

"Hah! Did my friend tell you that? Did you ask him how many human lives he wasted conducting the same experiments?"

I stared blankly at my father.

"Idiots like him believe that scientific progress is solely contingent on one's materials. Well, he can build as many hospitals and experiment on as many sick patients as he likes," he said, shaking his head, "but he will never get anywhere. Whereas a genius like K could get by with lab rats and rabbits alone."

"But do you have proof that K didn't murder his wife and child?

"I do. Indisputable proof."

"Which is?"

My father glanced at me significantly. I instinctively threw my hands over my head and felt a wide scar stretching from my forehead to the back of my skull.

"Father, am I K's son?"

"I didn't say that."

"Liar! You always wanted to experiment on me!"

My father looked away.

"Perhaps," he said in a low voice.

Chapter Twelve

TWO LITTLE DEATHS

I

It was a nice, warm spring day, and the sun was shining high in the sky, traveling west. Now and then, beautiful puffs of clouds sailed gently by like peach-colored boats on a calm blue sea. A flight of larks chased after the clouds, singing merrily to each other as higher and higher they climbed, till they scarcely could be seen at all.

The hospital on the edge of town was quiet; and quiet was the hospital garden, and the patients gazing at the flowers in the garden. In one of the rooms of the hospital lay a little Rich Boy. He was waiting for Death to come get him. Beside him lay a big Saint Bernard, his constant companion; a pair of yellow canaries sang him sweet songs from a cage; and a pretty vase of flowers filled the room with its fragrance.

From across the hall a little Poor Boy smiled at him. He was waiting for Death also, and had been, it would seem, since the day he was born. He had been waiting for Death when small and hanging at his sickly mother's breast; and later, when he had grown old enough to care for her himself, and work at the big factory with his father, was waiting for him still. So long had he been waiting, in fact, that everybody wondered why Death had not come for him already. "What is taking him so long?" they whispered to each other.

Now this little Poor Boy had no Saint Bernard to keep him company, no pair of yellow canaries to sing to him, and no pretty vase of flowers to scent his room; but when he saw how, like himself, the little Rich Boy looked out from his window at the bright, shining sun and the peach-colored clouds, he felt such brotherly love and kinship towards him that he began to see everything that the Rich Boy had as his own.

II

Drunk on the fragrance of spring, Death stalked the halls of the hospital. Her face was obscured by a long white veil, and she carried a sickle in her ice-cold hands . . .

"Everything must die," she said to herself. "The young and the old; the beautiful and the damned; the loved and the lost; the rich and the poor; the sage and the fool; the prince and the popper—all must die. It makes no difference to me. For I am an anarchist! I am an equalizer! I kill flowers and birds and men and women and children. Ah, what joy, what fun it is to reap destruction on living things! It is really quite invigorating."

Thus, spoke Death as she stalked the halls of the hospital. Her face was obscured by a long white veil, and she carried a sickle in her ice-cold hands . . .

But nobody minded. Her words were drowned out by the singing of larks, and the amorous whispering of spring winds.

Death entered the room of the little Poor Boy. The child was gazing at the blue of the sky, so he did not hear Death pass through the door.

"Turn around, little boy," said Death gravely. "It is time for you to die."

"Is it really?" wondered the child as he turned round. "Was I ever alive?"

"Were you not aware of that?"

"Not at all! In fact, today is the first day that I even suspected it."

"What a dim-witted child!" muttered Death to herself. "This is why I hate poor people. Why, they never seem to know whether they are living or dead. And they have no appreciation for life whatsoever. Really, I get no enjoyment from killing them at all!" Then, looking coldly down at the little Poor Boy, she said, "Listen, I will extend your insignificant life in exchange for that of your friend. Do we have a deal?"

"My friend?" asked the child.

"The boy across the hall," answered Death, directing the sharp point of her sickle towards the little Rich Boy, who was then looking out at the blue of the sky.

"But his life is his own," said the little Poor Boy. "It has nothing to do with me, and so it is not mine to give away."

"Don't get smart with me, little boy. Anything that you love is yours to give away, especially if I say it is."

"Really?" asked the child doubtfully.

"Yes, really," answered Death. "Now say that you will give it to me."

But the little Poor Boy just laughed.

"Ugh!" groaned Death, and she shook her sickle angrily. "Poor people!"

"Forgive me," said the child. "I am only laughing because I now realize that I am alive!"

"I don't care why you are laughing. Just say you will give me the little Rich Boy's life!"

"I am afraid I cannot do that," said the child. "For if what you say is true, and his life really does belong to me, then I will not hand it over to the likes of you. Rather, I will do everything in my power to protect it."

"I don't have time to argue semantics with you, little boy. Either you give me the life of your friend, or I take yours. Understood?"

"Then take mine," said the little Poor Boy, smiling.

"Ugh!" groaned Death. "Will you give me the life of his Saint Bernard at least?"

"The only life that you will get from me is my own."

"What about his canaries?"

"No."

"His flowers, then?"

"I am afraid not."

"Fine!" shouted Death. "Have it your way!" And she slipped out of the room.

"Ah!" said the little Poor Boy with delight. "How wonderful it is to know that I am alive! And I can feel it, right here in my heart. It is life that I feel. Oh joy!"

III

Death entered the room of the little Rich Boy. But once again, nobody minded, for they were all drunk on the comforts of spring, and dreaming their own sweet realities. The canaries were singing of faraway lands to their friend the Saint Bernard, who was only half-listening and half-plotting to swat a bothersome fly with his tail. The spring winds were whispering sweet-nothings to the vase of pretty flowers, and the little Rich Boy was gazing at the clouds sailing by like peach-colored boats on a calm blue sea.

"Turn around, little boy," said Death gravely. "It is time for you to die."

The child turned round, and his thin, small face became as white as a sheet.

"I beg you," he cried. "Let me live a while longer. Only a little while longer. Till I can no longer see those beautiful clouds in the sky; till the merciful sun has set in the west!"

"Spoiled brat!" scoffed Death. "You are in no position to bargain."

"Please!" implored the child. "Only let me see the larks return to their nests; only let me listen to end of the song that my canaries are singing!"

Death stood silent for a moment and thought. Then she smiled a faint, wicked smile.

"I will extend your life in exchange for the life of your flowers. Mind that anything you love is yours to give away."

"You may have it."

"And that of your canaries?"

"That also."

"And your Saint Bernard'?"

The little Rich Boy looked heartbroken.

"Look, I haven't all day," said Death peevishly. "I am a busy woman. Now, will you give me the dog's life, or no?"

"You may have it."

"And what about the life of your friend across the hall?"

The little Rich Boy scrunched up his face in pain.

"Give me his life," said Death, "and I will extend yours, till you can no longer see the beautiful clouds in the sky; till the merciful sun has set in the west."

"You may have it," murmured the child.

Then Death slipped out of the room, and the little Rich Boy buried his pale face in his pillow and wept.

IV

The next day a solemn funeral was held for the little Rich Boy. Family and friends stood round the magnificent coffin, which was covered in a large black pall, and strewn with many pretty flowers. Only the flowers were dead. The mourners looked on sorrowfully as the coffin was lowered into the cold, dark ground.

Around this time, the little Poor Boy was cremated. His bones were tossed into an unmarked box, to be shipped off somewhere—it does not matter where.

Nobody came to pay their respects, save for a young Nurse in a long white veil. She watched the box containing the remains of the little Poor Boy being carried out of the hospital, and her beautiful eyes filled with tears.

"I suppose that I should be going," she said to herself after a while. "Indeed, I really must be going"; and she walked off silently in the direction of the slums.

"Why, that woman looks just like Death!" murmured the Groundskeeper of the hospital as he watched her pass through the hospital gate. "She even has a long white veil and a silver sickle! Or did I imagine that?"

Chapter Thirteen

THE NARROW CAGE

I

The Tiger was tired . . .

Every day was the same . . .

There was his narrow cage, the narrow strips of sky between its bars, and all the other narrow cages stretching out round his own, as far as the eye could see . . . The rows of cages seemed to go on, one after the other, past the walls of the zoo, to the very ends of the earth.

Oh, how the Tiger was tired! So very tired indeed . . .

Every day was the same . . .

There were the fools who came to see him, their laughter, their nauseating stench . . .

"Ugh! if only I didn't have to look at those awful faces, or listen to that grating laughter!"

But the crowd of fools seemed to go on, one after the other, as far as the eye could see, past the walls of the zoo, to the very ends of the earth; and their laughter seemed capable of echoing until the end of time.

Oh, how the Tiger was tired! So very tired indeed . . .

He made himself small, like a kitten, and buried his face in his paws.

"Oh!" he exclaimed, trembling with disgust. "Must the life of a tiger consist of nothing more than looking at such ugly faces, than listening to such grating laughter?"

He heaved a heavy sigh of despair.

"Look!" shouted the people. "The tiger is crying!" and they rushed upon his cage from every direction.

The Tiger's whole body shook with fear and indignation, his tail beating violently against the bars and floor of his narrow cage.

He tried to remember a time when he was free and living in the jungle. There, at the foot of a great tree some thousands of years old, had stood a stone god all covered with flowers. People came from distant villages to kneel before the god, paying no mind at all to the Tiger's presence. They prayed with real devotion, now sighing, now watering the flowers with their tears. And the tears gamboled over the flowers, or sat pensively on the tips of their petals, glimmering strangely with the evening dew in the moonlight, like phosphorescent stones. Back then the Tiger used to make a game of trying to tell the tears apart from the dew.

One night he licked a teardrop that a man had shed before his god. He did not yet know that of all things offered up to God from man, there is nothing more precious than his tears.

One human teardrop did the Tiger taste, just one; and not long after that, he was caught. It seemed to him to be a punishment from the stone god.

The Tiger remembered and wept, and the more he wept the more his heart ached, till at last he folded his large paws in front of him like those men and women he had once seen praying to the stone god.

"Oh, God!" he cried out. "Would that you hide from me those ugly faces! Would that you quell that grating laughter!"

No sooner had the words left his mouth than did the laughter of the people begin to grow fainter and fainter, as if it were fading into the mists of a spring dream.

The Tiger's ears pricked up, and he listened. Somewhere he heard the murmur of a cool stream. Gone was the nauseating stench of man, the air having since grown heavy with the rich perfume of sweet-smelling flowers.

The Tiger started, and looked round him in astonishment. One can scarcely imagine the joy he must have felt at that moment, for his narrow cage and the crowd of fools had vanished without a trace. Once again he was alone in the jungle, at the foot of that great tree, in front of the stone god all covered with flowers, upon which teardrops still glimmered with a strange luster caught from the brilliant moonlight.

"Hurrah!" shouted the Tiger, leaping up. "I must have been dreaming!" and he danced about, proudly swinging his tail from side to side. His breast swelled with freedom, and every fiber of his body overflowed with power.

"What joy!" he said as he wandered aimlessly between the trees. "To think that I almost believed that my cage and those fools were real! Ah, but they were a dream, only a terrible dream. Truly there is nothing more hateful than a cage! That alone is what's real, and what I must keep with me till my dying day!"

II

Now leaping, now bounding, now rolling like a ball and throwing himself on the grass—how many miles the Tiger went he hardly knew. But just as he was going to enter a wide-open field, there seized upon him a very strange smell, and he stopped, his large nostrils quivering in their effort to identify it.

"Ah, sheep! There are sheep nearby. And yet I feel as though it has been a long time since I last smelled them . . ."

Following the scent of the sheep, the Tiger crawled through the long grass stealthily, so as not to make a sound.

Presently there appeared before him a high fence, and he could hear the sleepy cries of the sheep behind it. Surely the Tiger had seen fences like this before! Hundreds of times had he leapt over them to devour some unsuspecting prey! And yet tonight, when he looked at this fence, did his heart burn with unspeakable rage.

"This is a cage!" he seethed. "A narrow cage!" And he threw himself forward, growling more fearfully than thunder, slashing faster than lightning.

Against the full weight of his massive forepaws, the force of which was like a gale capable of destroying everything in its path, the thick posts of the fence began to waver, then collapse, one after the other, like a house of wooden blocks. Within minutes, a space large enough for a carriage to pass through had been cleared.

"Brothers and sisters!" cried the Tiger, still wreaking havoc upon the fence. "You are free! Free, I tell you! Now come out of your narrow cage!"

But the sheep only huddled together and trembled, there being nothing, it seemed to them, more terrifying than freedom.

The Tiger grew angry. "Slaves of man!" he roared. "Do you love this cage more than you love your freedom?"

He lunged into the middle of the herd and began tossing one sheep after another over the fence with his strong forepaws.

But the sheep came running back, bleating in the most piteous manner. To the Tiger it sounded as if their innards were being gouged with a knife.

Meanwhile the Shepherds looked on helplessly. Then, when they finally recovered themselves, they took up their rifles and fired a number of shots at the Tiger, two or three of which struck him in his side. At a safe distance, the sheepdogs growled, and prepared to attack should the opportunity avail itself.

"Damned sheep!" said the Tiger, spitting the words as though they were gobs of blood. "You are nothing but senseless beasts. You are lower than dogs. In fact, you are beyond salvation!" And he bounded into the jungle, and disappeared from sight.

He returned to the stone god, and made himself prostrate before it.

"Oh, God!" he cried out in prayer. "May I no longer hear the piteous cries of those sheep—the terrible cries of those slaves! They seem to echo to the very ends of the earth!" And he covered his ears with his forepaws and wept.

III

The Tiger was passing by the Rajah's summer palace. He had passed by it many times before, when embarking on long journeys to the bluff mountains of the Himalayas, or when loping about the dense and untouched jungles of Bengal; and many times had he cast a look of scorn upon its high stone walls and deep dark moat.

But this time, when he came to the front of the palace, he stopped, as one who is snared in a spell. His heart began to throb, and he felt something choking him in his throat.

"A cage . . ." he seethed. "A narrow cage . . ."

Inside the stately palace lived the Rajah's two hundred beautiful wives, who went about their luxurious lives in the finest silk fabrics. Oh, how the people of the village envied the lives of these women! Often, on their way back from the fields, did the young girls stop by the moat for a break; and after looking up at the palace for some time, would shoulder their straw baskets again, and set off for their poor huts, picturing to themselves, over and over, the brilliant and carefree world of the palace.

Ah! But what was this? The Tiger could plainly hear the heavy sighing of the Rajah's beautiful wives, yearning for freedom.

Framed by the green leaves of the trees, the round dome of the summer palace seemed to glitter like gold in the bright sunlight, while down below, the deep moat ran round the walls like a thick iron chain.

The Tiger had hated man his entire life, ever since he had clung to his mother's teat. And yet, for some reason, when he thought about the Rajah's wives being held captive in the palace, his heart began to throb, and his breathing became difficult.

He circled the palace a few times, then stopped in front of a large iron gate and stared vacantly across the moat, at the long drawn-up bridge on the other side.

All of a sudden, his ears picked up the sound of men approaching from the highway. So he dived into a bush, and crouching flat to the ground, held his breath and waited.

Presently there appeared through the trees a magnificent procession, in the midst of which rose two beautiful palanquins of wrought-gold, shouldered by slaves. In one of the palanquins sat the Rajah, and in the other, his latest bride-to-be. As the they passed by in august silence, neither seemed to notice the Tiger crouching in the bush.

The Tiger first studied the beaming face of the Rajah. Then he looked at the Rajah's bride-to-be. She was wrapped from head to toe in fine silks studded with precious stones. And though the lower portion of her face was hidden behind a veil, he was struck by the mild and sparkling light of her limpid sky-blue eyes.

The Tiger trembled.

"Those eyes," he said thoughtfully. "I have seen them before . . . But of course!" And he smiled a wry smile, for the woman's soft eyes were just like the eyes of the deer he had hunted many times in the fields.

As the Rajah's procession continued its march towards the palace, the drawbridge began to lower, and the gate opened. Inside the gate stood the Rajah's two hundred wives, laughing coyly behind their veils and awaiting the arrival of their lord.

Then, when the procession had crossed over, the bridge was drawn up, and the gate closed shut. Only the sound of a heavy lock falling into place resounded in the Tiger's ears.

■ ■ ■

The sun sank down behind the western hills, and the cries of the jungle signaled the coming of a sultry summer night. Framed by the dark-green leaves of the trees, the dome of the palace was enveloped by a purple mist.

The Tiger stood at the edge of the moat and gazed at the beckoning stone wall. What creature could hope to clear that moat, or scale that high stone wall?

The Tiger sighed.

"Oh! There are some things that even tigers cannot do!"

Suddenly he heard a sound from beyond the wall. It was the sound of someone being pursued, and of someone in pursuit.

The Tiger looked up and wondered. There, barefoot and dressed in her wedding finery, stood the veiled young Woman with the beautiful eyes. Through the evening mist, he could plainly see that she was trembling like a deer trembles when pursued by a tiger.

The Woman prepared to dive into the moat; but before she had bent both knees to spring, she noticed the Tiger staring at her with his strangely gleaming eyes. Instinctively, she started and drew back, at which point the Rajah seized her tightly by her wrist, and dragged her away like a tiger drags a deer away in its maw.

The Woman screamed, and for a split-second the Tiger's mind went blank. His whole body felt as though it were on fire.

He dove into the moat.

A few minutes later he appeared at the top of the wall, where he paused a moment before dropping down into the Rajah's pleasure garden.

In the Rajah's garden all was still and quiet—save for the murmuring of a fountain and the whispering of the flowers.

The Tiger felt his rage subsiding. He stopped to sniff the evening air, which was heavy with the delicate perfume of flowers. It seemed tainted by the stench of man. After taking a few more sniffs, he picked out the scent he was looking for.

He leaped onto a veranda and peered behind a velvet curtain. There was a large and empty chamber behind it. He crept in and looked round.

The chamber glittered with the eerie light of many marvelous weapons and jewels. In one corner, on a marble stand, stood a large glass bowl, in which a Goldfish was playing in the moonlight. In another corner was an elegantly wrought cage, in which a Canary was sleeping soundly on its perch.

"A cage!" growled the Tiger, his rage rekindled. "A narrow cage! Everywhere I go, there are more narrow cages!" And he bounded off towards the bird cage.

"You!" he yelled at the Canary, shaking the cage with his forepaws. "Get out of there this instant! Fly away and be free! The jungle is awash with moonlight! It awaits your return!"

The Canary started awake and immediately flew to the corner of his cage.

"Can't you see?" continued the Tiger. "I am here to free you. Now fly from your narrow cage. Fly away and be free!"

But the Canary could not think of anything more terrifying than freedom.

"Slave of man!" shouted the Tiger. "Be free, I say!" And he stuck his paw into the cage and tried to pull out the bird. But when he pulled out his paw, he saw that the bird was dead.

For a time the Tiger sat silent in a pool of silver moonlight.

"The poor thing," he said softly. "It may have been a slave, but it was still beautiful." And laying the cold body of the Canary on the brightest tile of the chamber, he bounded off towards the Goldfish in the fishbowl.

The Goldfish was blowing bubbles and rolling over to expose her belly to the moon.

"Goldfish, little Goldfish" said the Tiger gently. "Let me take you away to the great and beautiful Ganges. The water is more beautiful there. Let me set you free in the great and limitless ocean. The moon is more beautiful there."

But the Goldfish was so startled to see a Tiger standing in front of him that she sank to the bottom of her bowl. She could not think of anything more terrifying than the Ganges, nothing more disquieting than the great and limitless ocean.

"You are a slave!" shouted the Tiger. "You are all slaves of man!" and he stuck his right forepaw into the water and tried to seize the Goldfish. But the Goldfish kept slipping through his grasp, as if to taunt him.

Growing more enraged, the Tiger rose up on his haunches, and thrust both forepaws into the water. But the Goldfish continued to evade him.

"Senseless beast!" he growled. "Slave of man!" he spat.

Then he upset the fishbowl, and it fell to the floor with a deafening crash.

A curtain at the back of the chamber was torn aside, and the Rajah rushed in, dressed in his nightgown and clutching a pistol. For a moment—for one brief moment—his eyes met with the narrow, raging eyes of the Tiger . . .

There sounded a gunshot, a roar that shook the foundations of the palace and the cry of a man clinging desperately to his life.

After that, all was silent once more—save for the cool murmuring of the fountain and the soft whispering of the flowers . . .

Upon the moonlit floor of the chamber, the Goldfish flapped, gasping for air, while the Rajah's two hundred and one wives looked on with bated breath.

IV

The Tiger lay down in front of the stone god, and, for the length of a day, licked the wound in his breast. His body smarted all over, yet he shed no tears. Only now and then did he heave a heavy sigh of despair.

He did not pray to the stone god, but sank into dark thoughts. He would not be like man, he swore. He would not pray to the stone god for salvation.

Another sultry summer night arrived, casting its mantle over everything. Jackals howled forebodingly in the distance. The Tiger tried to sleep, but the screeching of unseen birds would not let him. The noises troubled him deeply.

He looked up.

"What's that?" he said, straining his ears and nostrils. "Someone has come to pray. No, not some *one*, but many. Many men are coming."

He sniffed a more delicate scent.

"Ah!" he gasped. "I know that scent. But whose is it? Not Jim the Hunter; nor Anand the Woodcutter; nor Rama the Fakir. Oh! I know it! It is that woman who reminds me of a deer! But wait—I smell the Rajah also. Impossible. I shattered his skull into four pieces! I am sure of that. And there are Brahmins with them. One, two . . . What could they be up to? Some secret meeting? Or perhaps they intend to burn that woman alive. Oh, God, they are going to burn her along with the body of the Rajah!"

The Tiger trembled.

"I won't allow it!" he went on. "They mustn't touch a hair on that woman's head." And he hid himself behind a bush and peered out through the leaves.

Just then, a soft wind blew from the opposite direction, and the Tiger's nostrils were filled with yet another scent.

"What's this? More men! And gunpowder too. Why, it's a sepoy army! And there is a white man with them. An official . . . They are trying to surround the area. But for what? It seems as if they are trying to apprehend someone. Surely they are not out hunting. There are too many of them for that. There must be over a hundred men."

Presently a magnificent funeral procession of about twenty or thirty people, led by a group of Brahmins, stopped in front of the stone god. The Brahmins and their attendants were all trembling, fearing lest they should make the slightest noise. They looked round with the most frightened expressions.

The Woman Who Resembled a Deer was looking anxiously into the jungle, and the Tiger imagined that she was waiting for somebody who would come and rescue her from the clutches of the Brahmins.

"She is waiting for me," he smiled, "though she knows it not."

Then the slaves set themselves to work, and within ten minutes had erected a large funeral pyre in the middle of the glade.

Meanwhile the Woman prayed, and it seemed to all who were present that her prayer would last an eternity.

This irritated the Brahmins and their attendants very much. "Enough!" they shouted finally. "The sacred fire awaits! Deva awaits! She demands your innocent soul!

The slaves laid the Raja's coffin on the pyre.

But the Woman continued to pray, and with her helpless eyes she called out to somebody across the Indian summer night.

The Tiger watched her, smiling.

The small eyes of the Brahmins glinted sharply in their pinched faces.

"Enough!" they shouted. "Queen Deva awaits your sacrifice! This is your final obligation to the gods!"

The slaves watched for a sign to light the pyre, and the flames of their torches licked the night air with red, snake-like tongues.

The Woman was casting one last look into the jungle when two Brahmins seized her. As she was being pulled towards the pyre, the Tiger could clearly make out the Woman's pallid face beneath her veil.

Then the Brahmins began to intone a strange prayer while the slaves lit the pyre from all sides. Thin wisps of smoke rose into the night like a dying breath.

The Tiger's mind went blank, and he prepared to leap out of his covert, when all of a sudden, scores of sepoy infantry darted out.

The Brahmins and their attendants were thunderstruck. A cry of joy broke from the Woman's lips, and it seemed to echo all the way to the Himalayas.

"It was not me she was waiting for," winced the Tiger, clutching his breast with his forepaws, as if to stop it from breaking. "It was the White Man . . ."

Waving a strange paper in the air, the White Man began issuing orders. Then he took the Woman down from the pyre and clasped her tightly in his arms.

The Brahmins looked on, their eyes flashing. With a mixture of fear and indignation, they turned to face the stone god.

"Gods of India!" they cried, lifting their hands into the air. "Divine protectors of our lands! This faithless woman hath betrayed thee. May she suffer eternal damnation for the evil she hath wrought! For she hath fallen for the enemy! The enemy of India! May she be cursed for betraying us Brahmins, who act only in thy name!"

The attendants repeated the words like an echo.

" . . . May she be cursed!"

The Woman began to tremble. But the White Man was firm and held her closer to him. He looked into her eyes, his face full of pride, and he whispered something. The Tiger strained his ears to hear it and thought that he heard him whisper words of love.

At length the sepoys led the slaves, the Brahmins, and their attendants away. And the White Man and the Woman disappeared with them, into the jungle like a midsummer nights' dream.

Thin wisps of smoke rose into the sky like a dying breath.

V

The Tiger rose to all fours, his chest throbbing with an excruciating pain, his brain raging with a fever the likes of which he had never felt before. Soundlessly, so as to go unseen by the stone god and everyone else, he slunk through the jungle in pursuit of the men who had but a moment ago vanished like a midsummer night's dream.

The silence of the night deepened. The innumerable leaves of the jungle were sleeping peacefully, awash in the radiant moonlight.

All of a sudden, that silence was broken by a scream, a volley of gunshots, and a tumult of confused voices. A shadow rippled across the trees at a speed that was faster than the wind.

After that, the silence of the night resumed.

The Tiger returned to his previous spot in the jungle glade, and the trail he walked was stained with blood.

Out of the corner of his eye he caught a glimpse of the stone god.

"Humph," he grunted. "He knows nothing. And what if he did? There is but one less white man in the world."

Not having the courage to face the stone god, the Tiger crawled beneath a bush.

Under the black mantle of night, all was quiet. Jackals howled in the distance, announcing the arrival of midnight.

The Woman Who Resembled a Deer came running to where the stone god stood, her white veil trailing behind her, her disheveled hair falling all over a bloodless face, in which were set two limpid eyes of utter sadness. In her trembling hands she held a silver dagger.

She knelt before the stone god and endeavored to pray, but all the prayers she had once known, she had now forgotten. Surely the stone god would never forget that face, which, lit by light of the moon, was the face of one who had forgotten how to pray.

The Woman tried to recall a single word of prayer, but she could recall nothing.

"Oh!" she wailed bitterly. "I have been cursed by my gods! I have betrayed the will of the Brahmins. I have fallen for the enemy of my people, the enemy of the gods of my people, and now I have nowhere to go but hell!" And she plunged the dagger into her heart.

The Tiger groaned as though the dagger had in fact been plunged into his own heart, and he leaped out of the bush.

The Woman lay before him in a heap. He lifted up her head up with one paw, and with the other pulled the dagger from her breast.

As always, the stone god stood perfectly still. All around it, the flowers were stained with fresh blood—the Woman's final offering.

The Tiger watched the light go out of the Woman's eyes, and he began to think. He thought about how man must live in some invisible, indestructible cage. And the more he thought, the more he became filled with rage.

"Man is nothing but a slave!" he roared. "He is nothing but a senseless beast! But who is it that has put him in his cage?"

The Tiger looked at the stone god.

"No, not him," he snarled. "He knows nothing. But then, who?"

The blood on the flowers mingled with the evening dew, shining marvelously in the moonlight like precious stones. They looked like the beads of a necklace worn by some angel come down from Heaven.

"The blood of slaves shines brighter than rubies," murmured the Tiger. "But how does it taste?" And again he looked at the stone god. "He will not know," he went on. "Not if I only taste one drop, one single drop . . ."

So he licked a drop of the slavish blood that lay glimmering on the flowers like so many precious stones.

And the ruby-red blood and the stone god faded away; and the murmuring of the cool stream and the whispering of the green leaves were gradually replaced by the voices of men and women and children; and the delicate fragrance of the flowers turned stale and was replaced by the nauseating stench of man.

The Tiger opened his eyes. He was curled up in the center of a narrow cage. Everywhere he looked, he saw still more narrow cages, stretching out as far as the eye could see. And all around him were ugly faces.

"Ah! But of course!" howled the Tiger. "This narrow cage and these ugly faces—they were real all along!"

"Look!" shouted the people. "The Tiger is roaring!"

The Tiger leapt to his feet, and with the full force of his strength, he threw himself against the iron bars of his cage. But he could not break them. He let out a fearful roar and tried again, but this time he knocked his head against the bars and fell to the floor bleeding.

At first the people ran away in fear, but then, when they saw the Tiger quivering on the floor, they came back and jeered at him.

"Oh!" moaned the Tiger, shutting his eyes. "Those ugly faces! That grating laughter!" and he cried one last time to the stone god.

"Oh, God! Take my blood as a final offering! Only hide from me these ugly faces and quell this grating laughter!"

No sooner than the words left his mouth did the laughter fade away, replaced by the stillness of a sultry summer night, and the stench of the human crowd softened into the delicate fragrance of the primeval jungle.

But the Tiger did not open his eyes—not to look at the beautiful glade, nor the stone god, nor the great tree, nor the slavish blood gleaming like rubies in the moonlight. He did not open his eyes again. He no longer had the will to do so.

PART II

Chinese Tales (1921–1923)

Chapter Fourteen

FROM "TALES OF A WITHERED LEAF"

SHANGHAI SKETCHES

Dedicated to my dear friends in China

INTRODUCTION

It was cold; it was Autumn; my very first Autumn in Shanghai, and memories of the springtime in Japan—of dear friends and never-ending excitements—made it colder still and sadder. I was very lonely when I first arrived in this unfamiliar city.

Fortunately, I soon ran into two friends whom I had known in Japan, and who had arrived sometime before me. They were lonely too, so we clung to each other fast.

China was to us a mystery—one that we had neither the desire nor the energy to solve. My thoughts drifted to Europe, while their dreams chased the South China Sea and Tibet. We feared our Ferry of Happiness had been shipwrecked, never to sail again. Stranded on the desert island of Shanghai, we had neither the strength to rebuild our ferry, nor the courage to think of China as our new home. Strangers to this noisy desert island, we hopelessly looked out at the swelling sea of people around us.

Often did we walk through the large market, where thousands of men and women bought and sold, cheated and were cheated. Accompanied by the incessant din of human life, we, with smiles on our faces, and unbearable pain in our hearts, would exclaim to each other: "Surely this is an impassable forest!"

Wandering in this "New World,"[1] how often did we repeat to each other: "Why does man seek solitude in the mountains when he could just as well find it in the New World? Here one feels more alone than if one were lost in the Himalayas!"

One day, while wandering about aimlessly, we came upon a large old tree, stripped of its bark, and with one withered leaf still clinging to it. The sight of this lonely survivor impressed us deeply. We stood speechless before it; but from our ever-smarting hearts there arose a thousand questions. Oh, how we pitied that leaf, for we ourselves were as pitiful as it; and we listened, motionless, as it seemed to be saying: "I did everything to remain on this Tree; I loved no one but myself, my sole aim being to keep from falling. And lo! Now I am alone and cold and withering, thinking I never did anything, never loved anyone . . ."

---

[1] Author's note: "The New World" is the largest entertainment district in Shanghai, in which can be found theaters, bars, gambling dens, etc.

The leaf fell on my hat, and I carried it home with me.

Now on cold Autumn nights—such lonely, sleepless nights—when, with my face buried in my pillow, I try to hold back my tears and grief for my shipwrecked Ferry of Happiness, the withered Leaf appears before me and tells me many tales. Listening to it speak, I begin to forget about my Ferry of Happiness, which I shipwrecked by my own hand, till I am no longer sorry for it, and weep for it no longer.

Even if everything should turn out to be a dream, and I wake up to find myself still in my Ferry of Happiness, I shall not change its course, nor move its rudder one bit. Indeed, I shall go straight to the sea where I am destined to perish.

But here are some tales that the withered leaf told me. And should they excite some happy thoughts in you, dear reader, or stir some noble sentiments in your heart, then its life will not have been in vain, and I will have accomplished my authorial task.

I

THE TREE IN THE STREET

I know of a Tree on a street in this city. Now it stands silent; now it says nothing; nothing it wants now to say. And I know not the number of years it has lived, though I know it has witnessed the glory of emperors, and also their ruin and shame.

It has witnessed the people of this land dispossessed by their very own high-ranking thieves. It has witnessed the people of this land dispossessed by foreign-born low-ranking thieves. It has cried to the Wind, saying, "Wind, blow me down, that I might see no more!" But the Wind loved the Tree, for the Tree was so old.

Now it watches the people dispossessed by their own, dispossessed by another, be they yellow or white; but it speaks not a word; it has nothing to say—wherefore I know not at all.

It has witnessed the people kneeling down in the mud to worship their great men and elders. It has witnessed the people kneeling down in the dust at the foreign-born butchers' command. It has cried to the Men who were cutting down trees to make room for the white man's new world, saying, "Men, cut me down! You must cut me down fast! That I might see no more of these devils and demons; that I might see no more of these poor slavish people and their more slavish leaders!" But the Men only bowed, for the Tree was so old.

Now it watches the people lying down in the mud, rolling round in the dust, as they worship the butchers from near and from far; but it speaks not a word; it has nothing to say—wherefore I know not at all.

It has witnessed the coming of grandiose streets, and the building of homes for the wealthy exploiters, and the planning of parks that the people can't walk in. It has cried in despair, saying, "What has become of my beautiful people? And what has become of my glorious land? Is its spirit now dead? Has its soul now departed? Will its heart beat no more in the breasts of the Youth?" But nobody answered, for nobody knew. So the Tree became silent; it spoke not a word, there was nothing it wanted to say.

Now it watches the Children, who begin playing sports, and who end playing war, or perhaps playing cards, laying down on the table their very last dollar, along with their honor; and it watches the Youth, who begin drinking wine, and who end smoking pipes; and it watches the Elders, who begin selling thoughts, and who end selling land . . . And it speaks not a word; it has nothing to say—wherefore I know not at all.

II

THE ISLE OF DREAMS

It was spring, and the young Leaves of the old Tree were singing green hymns to the sun, to the warm, dreamy Nights, to the magical Moon, and the enigmatic Stars . . .

They were trembling with joy; they were trembling with love; and life rushed through all of their little leaf-veins.

And they called to the Tree, saying, "Tell us, old Tree; tell us how should we love? And whom should we love while we live?"

But the Tree made no answer; it spoke not a word. And the green Leaves felt sad as they trembled with joy, as they trembled with love.

It was night—and the magical Moon was bewitching the world, and the enigmatic Stars were scattering puzzles all over the heavens.

And mischievous Dreams were invading the Earth, pulling childish pranks on kings in their castles and on shepherds in their fields.

The silent night deepened . . .

The Southern Breeze slept on its way to the river, the Magnificent River, to the city that was built in the white man's new style; it had fallen asleep having left the South Sea, while the mischievous Dreams were invading the Earth.

Rang the Clock-Tower, which sleeps not a wink, even on dreamy spring nights like this.

And the Southern Breeze woke all at once with a start.

"Was that a Spring Dream?" it exclaimed as it woke; but the Dreams had flown off, and they laughed as they went.

"Oh, Spring Dreams," cried the Breeze, "you must wait. You must answer me something!" But the Dreams had flown off, and they laughed as they went.

So the Southern Breeze flew, chasing after the Dreams on its swift southern wings, crying, "Wait, you Spring Dreams! You must answer me, please!"

But those mischievous Dreams—they had hidden themselves in the little green Leaves of the silent old Tree.

Then the Southern Breeze came, and it said to the Tree, "Good Tree with green leaves, pray, wither have flown all the Dreams of the Spring?"

But the old Tree stood silent, while the Dreams smiled within, and the little green Leaves all trembled with laughter.

So the Breeze kissed the Leaves, pleading: "Tell me, green Leaves! Tell me, green little brothers, wither have flown all the Dreams of the Spring?"

And the green Leaves made jest, saying, "We do not know, for we cannot see. But perhaps they have flown to the bright Southern Cross?"

How the green Leaves believed that the Dreams of the Spring would stay with them always, forever and ever!

And the Spring Dreams all smiled.

And the old Tree stood silent.

So the Breeze went on pleading, saying, "Listen, green Leaves! Listen, green little brothers, I have just had a vision of the Isle of Dreams. It lies on the Sea of Everlasting Love, and its port is the Port of Immutable Friendship, into which flows the River of Joy. And there blooms the Flower of Loyalty, and there grows the Tree of Virtue; and there rises the Mountain of Liberty, over which shines the Sun of Truth, the Moon of Justice, and the Stars of Fine Arts . . . Oh, the wonders of this place are many indeed. So you must come with me, my green little brothers. You must come with me to the Isle of Dreams!"

"But the way—do you know it?" demanded the Leaves. "You must tell us right now! You must tell us this instant!"

"Ah, the way . . ." sighed the Breeze, "I'm afraid I don't know it, so I must ask the Dreams, but they've all flown away . . ."

And the green Leaves cried out, "Why, the Dreams are right here, hiding in this old Tree! You must ask them the way to the Isle of Dreams!"

But the mischievous Dreams were not there anymore, they had all flown away. And they laughed at the Breeze and the Leaves as they went.

And the old Tree stood silent.

So the green Leaves felt doubt in their little leaf-veins, and they spoke to the Tree, saying, "Tell us, old Tree; tell us, are we to trust the sweet words of the Breeze? And are we to put all our faith in the Dreams, when the magical Moon is bewitching the world, and the enigmatic Stars are scattering puzzles all over the heavens?"

But the Tree made no answer. It did not want to say that the Dreams had flown off to the faraway North, to the land of the Snow and the world-turning Spirit. It did not want to say that the Dreams had no fear of the Cold or the Frost. It did not want to say how the people of the North always wanted to dream.

And the Southern Breeze cried, saying, "Leaves, we must go! Oh, my green little brothers! I can feel it, the Isle of Dreams is nearby!"

"But we don't feel a thing," said the little green Leaves. "Does it really exist?"

And the Southern Breeze answered: "If it does not exist, we will build it ourselves!"

"But how?" asked the Leaves. "Tell us, how can we build such an Isle of Dreams, with its gold Sun of Truth, and its silver Moon of Justice?"

And the Southern Breeze answered: "With the Spirit of Youth! For the Spirit of Youth is the source of all power. It is God the Creator—once, now, and forever!"

Said the Leaves: "Tell us, Tree! Shall we put all our trust in the Spirit of Youth?"

But the old Tree stood silent, and made them no answer.

So some Leaves cried out, saying, "We will never go searching for the Isle of Dreams; we will never go anywhere; we will never depart from our native branches!"

But the old Tree stood silent.

So the Southern Breeze left on its swift southern wings . . .

It was dawn . . .

III

THE GIRL AND HER SECRET

It was spring, and the young Leaves of the old Tree were trembling with love and joy. And the whole world was smiling: the blue Sky, the proud Sun, and the strange little Clouds searching for happiness in the infinite heavens . . .

There came to the Tree a nine-year-old girl. She too was smiling; she too was trembling with love and joy; and her eyes were shining with a secret hope.

She said: "Good Tree with green leaves, is it true man is mortal? And if so, does that mean that my brother must die? No, certainly not. For my brother is twelve. And must twelve-year-old boys die because man is mortal?

"Good Tree with green leaves, I love only him. I have no one else. I hate all the others, who, to bury my father, sold my first-eldest sister; and to bury my mother, sold my second-eldest sister. Now they want to sell me, to hire a doctor to treat my sick brother. But my brother will never allow that to happen!

"Good Tree with green leaves, when daughters are sold, who is it that buys them? My brother has said that our dear older sisters were bought to be sold again, night after night. Is that true, what he said? I have often desired to visit the place where daughters are sold, but no one is willing to show me the way . . .

"Good Tree with green leaves, is it really so bad to cough up some blood? They all say that my brother must not leave his room, must not play with friends, must not read or write; must not talk too much; that he must lie in bed or sit in his chair in front of the window. How sad he is then! For outside the window are dirty brick walls. Oh, why do they build such dirty brick walls? Are they trying to hide all the world and its wonders?

"Good Tree with green leaves, they forbid me to see him; they forbid us to play; they forbid me to lay down my head on his knees. They say I'm too old. But how can I live so apart from my brother? I love only him; he loves only me; we hate all the others, who, to bury our father, sold off one sister, and, to bury our mother, sold off another . . .

"Good Tree with green leaves, I will tell you a secret. You must tell it to no one, not the Wind nor the Clouds . . .

"As soon as it's dark and the house is asleep, I stealthily creep to the room of my brother. And I lie in his bed; and I sleep in his arms; and I give little kisses to his pale blemished face . . .

"And then I am happy, and all is forgotten.

"We tell each other stories: about God and His Angels, and our parents who fly among beautiful stars; about monsters in the sea and devils in the hills; about little crafty foxes and big scary wolves; about all the strange white men who live in our city . . .

"And under the covers, we play many games, or else we admire the pictures in books. And when I feel tired, I lie in his arms till the Clock-Tower wakes us. Then I stealthily creep on back to my room, where I wait for my uncles and aunties to rise . . .

"Good Tree with green leaves, you must not tell my secret; you must tell it to no one, not the Wind nor the Clouds . . .

"I too have coughed blood, but nobody knows this. I've coughed it in secret and hid the red spittle, or if someone was near, I swallowed it down. And lo! I am happy; I walk about freely and play with my friends, while my poor older brother must lie in his bed, or sit by the window, and look out at nothing but dirty brick walls.

"Oh, why must they build such dirty brick walls?

"But the worst thing of all is that, day after day, my brother must drink the most terrible drink. Oh, good Tree with green leaves, am I to believe a disease of the lungs can be cured with such things? All the others say yes, but my brother says no. With tears does he drink it. But he drinks it no longer. I drink it instead. For each night, when we play games of cards in his bed, he declares that the loser must drink all the drink. And because he is clever, he wins every game. So I drink all the drink; and oh, how he laughs then!

"But our uncles and aunties suspect not a thing. For my brother is careful, my brother is wise. Indeed, he often amazes my uncles and aunties . . .

"Good Tree with green leaves, is it true that wise children don't live very long? Then is old-age for fools? Why, that would be awful. Both of my grandparents lived to be ninety, yet many have said that they were quite wise. To what age will our uncles and aunties live, then, for nobody says they're a little bit wise . . .

"Now I beg you, good Tree, give me some of your leaves, out of which I might weave a green crown for my brother . . ."

And she stretched out her hands.

And the green Leaves exclaimed, saying, "Tell us, old Tree, are we to take pity on this seedling that man calls a 'little girl'?"

But the old Tree stood silent, and made them no answer.

So the green Leaves grew sad, and many cried out: "We will never trust anyone; we will never go anywhere; we will never depart from our native branches!"

But some branches bent down, and shook off their Leaves. And the Girl took them up and wove a green crown. Then she went her way home, where her brother lay waiting with a pale blemished face.

He was already dead . . .

And the old Tree stood silent, and spoke not a word. It did not want to tell how the green crown was placed on a cold, thoughtless head; it did not want to tell how the Girl was sold off for to bury her brother.

And the whole world was smiling: the blue Sky, the proud Sun, and the strange little Clouds searching for happiness in the infinite heavens . . .

IV

THE HORSE-MAN

The Spring was now over. Kissed many times by the hot Summer Sun, the Leaves of the Tree began to turn gold. They no longer sang hymns; they were terribly tired. The love and the joy of the beautiful spring seemed a fast-fading dream. And doubt and regret filled their yellowing veins as they hung in the still, sultry air.

As always, the old Tree stood silent. There was nothing it wanted to say.

There came to the Tree a certain young Man. He had every right to be happy; but not suspecting his youth, had forgotten his rights. He embraced the Tree firmly, and pressed his hot cheek to its freezing-cold trunk.

It was night-time. No Stars were shining, and the Moon had forgotten the Earth. It was excessively hot. No Wind was stirring, and the Leaves hung heavy in the sultry air.

With his cheek pressed against the Tree, the young Man stood silent. He seemed to be searching for something to say.

At last he cried out: "Good Tree with gold leaves, how long must I serve as the rich people's horse? How long must I serve as their low beast of burden? Till I'm coughing up blood? Till the lungs in my chest are completely destroyed? Well, that time has arrived: for I'm coughing up blood, and little remains of my pulverized lungs.

"Good Tree with gold leaves, how long must I suffer the blows of the riders? Till they've knocked out my teeth to prevent me from biting? Till my voice has grown hoarse, and I no longer bark at those so-called progressives and their 'wonderous' white culture? Well, that time has arrived: for they've knocked out my teeth to prevent me from biting; and my voice has grown hoarse from weeping and sighing!"

And he opened his fist, and the Leaves saw white teeth all covered in blood. And the Tree looked and witnessed his bloody red mouth; but it spoke not a word; it only stood silent.

So the young Man went on: "Good Tree with gold leaves, how long must I suffer a life without light, a life without warmth, a life without air? Till my heart bursts with hate for the whole human race, and explodes in mad curses at Heaven and the gods who created the world, and the people who live in the world, for making life Hell?

"Good Tree with gold leaves, never in life or in dreams had I soft hands to hold; but how many hands—be they yellow or white, be they young or old-aged—have beaten me! Never in life or in dreams had I even a flaming mouth to kiss; but how many mouths—be they familiar or foreign, be they female or male—have spat on me with disdain! Oh, good Tree with gold leaves, have pity on this horse-man, have pity on this rikshaw-driver, who has the whole human race to hate, but only your cold trunk to love."

And the gold Leaves exclaimed, saying, "Tell us, old Tree, are we to take pity on this seedling that man calls a 'rikshaw-driver'?"

But the old Tree stood silent, and made them no answer.

So the gold Leaves grew sad, and many cried out: "Man can do as he pleases! We will not intervene! We will never depart from our native branches!"

But some Leaves tumbled down on the young Man's stiff shoulders, and they spoke to him softly of the rights of all people: to be happy, to be loved . . .

It was night-time. No Stars were shining, and the Moon had forgotten the Earth.

The very next morning, the Man was found dead and embracing the Tree with gold leaves. In his tightly-clenched fist were some bloody white teeth, which had recently been knocked out of his bloody red mouth.

The Man's cause of death was never discovered. Not that any one cared. For none would have guessed that his poor heart had burst with hatred for the whole human race and its wonderous white culture, with an anger towards Heaven and the gods who created the world, and the people who live in the world, for making life Hell. He knew nothing of that, for the Tree had said nothing; there was nothing it wanted to say . . .

V

THE WOMAN WITH LITTLE FEET

Autumn came, and the gold Leaves turned red. The hot kisses of the Summer Sun had become, like the Spring, a fast-fading dream. The listless world was awaiting the listless Winter; and its hopes and dreams had all flown off to the Land of Reminiscence.

As always, the old Tree stood silent.

There came to the Tree a young Woman with sweat on her brow and tears in her eyes. Hardly could she walk, her feet were too small and dainty. From the day of her birth, her family had decided that her feet should charm men, not walk on city streets.

The young Woman sat under the old Tree and wept.

And the old Tree stood silent.

But the red Leaves all trembled as they looked over the weeping seedling, the young Woman who could hardly walk on her small, dainty feet.

The Woman sobbed: "Good Tree with red leaves, have pity on this Woman with little bound feet: these feet that can't walk; this heart that won't beat! Have pity on these feet all covered in dust, all covered in blood. On these little bound feet did I come all the way from the faraway Mountains. There was I born, and there I expected to die. There did the Mountains teach me to love—to love a young Man, courageous and true, a child of the Mountains, a brother of the Rocks, a friend to the Eagles.

"Our parents betrothed us at a very young age, and together with him did I learn to love the Mountains, and to fear the Magnificent River, the enigma of the world—the mysterious Yangtze. Every morning, when the sun would softly redden the snowy peaks of the Mountains, would I thank them for my beloved, and bless their snowy peaks for my happiness; and every evening, when the parting rays of the Sun had received their last commissions, would I bless once again the Mountains for my courageous hero, for my mountainous love. This I did every morning and evening; save but one day . . .

"Good Tree with red Leaves, it was only one day! One day did I forget to give thanks for my hero, for my mountainous love. I remember it well. I was standing beside him on a high rock, looking out at the rays of the sun as they bid farewell to the Earth. He was looking at me—Not at me, but my feet. 'Promise me,' he said, 'that you'll always be happy, that you'll always laugh sweetly in these beautiful mountains.'

" 'I promise,' I answered. "If I cannot be happy on these beautiful Mountains, then where can I hope to be happy?' He said once again: 'Promise me that you'll never, for whatever reason, go to the Magnificent River, to the enigma of the world—to the mysterious Yangtze!' 'I promise,' I answered, 'Never shall I go to the Magnificent River!'

"And he carefully helped me down from the rock, and . . . Oh, at that moment I thanked both my parents for binding my feet; and I blessed both my feet for making me helpless. At that ill-fated moment I forgot to give thanks to the Mountains for my hero, for my mountainous love. And this all because I was thanking my parents for my little bound feet.

"Good Tree with red leaves, it was only one moment! And the very next morning, when the sun hailed the Mountains, he was gone.

"But where did he go? And why did he leave? No one would tell me, but everyone stared at my little bound feet. Many months did I weep, many months did I doubt and try to make sense of why he had gone. And at length I decided that I should go too.

"So I kissed the firm Rocks, said farewell to the Eagles, and shed tears of parting to the peaks of the Mountains.

"I went straight to the river, the Magnificent River. For I knew he was there; I knew it, I felt it, my heart had assured me. He had gone to the city that was built for white people, where he lived among devils from near and from far.

"Good Tree with red leaves, on these little bound feet did I walk the long road from the faraway Mountains to the white people's city; and had the road been a hundred-times longer, or a thousand-times more difficult, I still would have walked it on these little bound feet. For I believed that my hero would be waiting at the end, along with my happiness. My heart told me so, it swore this to me. But my heart told a lie . . .

"Good Tree with red leaves, I did not find my hero, that child of the Mountains, that brother of the Rocks, that friend of the Eagles. In his stead I found a Man with an ever-pale face, an ever-weary mien, ever-dull eyes, and ever-trembling lips. His

CHINESE TALES (1921-1923)

head was weighed down by thoughts of making money; and his breast only beat when it looked upon gold. For riches, he had given up everything noble: the honesty of the Mountains, the loyalty of the Rocks; the bravery of the Eagles. And a slavish fear of poverty reigned over his heart . . .

"Oh, Magnificent River, enigma of the world, mysterious Yangtze! What have you done to my hero of the Mountains, to that brother of the Rocks, to that friend of the Eagles? Are there not enough slaves in this land as it is? Are there not enough money-loving beasts on your shores? Are there not enough covetous brutes in your cities?

"Good Tree with red leaves, he said that my feet were not suited for walking The Hard Road of Life; he told me that Women with such little feet were not suited for fighting The Hard Fight of Life. Was he right? You are old; you know best. Oh, tell me, are my little bound feet not suited for The Hard Road of Life or The Hard Fight of Life?"

The Woman looked up with tears in her eyes.

But the old Tree stood silent, and made her no answer.

Then the red Leaves exclaimed, saying, "Tell us, good Tree, are we to take pity on this little-footed seedling?"

But the Tree kept its silence. It spoke not one word. And the Leaves trembled sadly, and many cried out: "We will never know how and whom we should pity! We will never depart from our native branches!"

But some Leaves tumbled down on the young Woman's feet, all covered in dust, all covered in blood. And they whispered to the Woman from the faraway Mountains and told her that to walk on The Hard Road of Life one needed not big feet but a great big heart; that to fight The Hard Fight of Life one needed not tigers' paws nor stallions' hooves, but a decisive will, a just spirit, and a full knowledge of the world!

The Woman stood up, and said with decision: "Good Tree with red leaves, I lack all these things. I am only a girl, the most ordinary girl of the faraway Mountains. And all that I have are these little bound feet, which do not want to walk, and this heart, which does not want to beat. And so I will go to the Magnificent River. And if that enigma, the mysterious Yangtze, does not grant me happiness, at least it will grant me repose in its waves. So I ask you, good Tree with red leaves—nay, I beg you, have the Wind send my final farewell to the faraway Mountains and their snowy white peaks; and then have it send my first and last kiss to that Man with the ever-pale face, and the ever-weary mien and ever-trembling lips. But don't let him know of my little bound feet and where they are headed . . ."

And she went away.

And the old Tree stood silent, and the red Leaves cried out, saying, "Tell us, good Tree, did that seedling go away to the Magnificent River? Is she some sort of water-plant?"

But the Tree made no answer.

The very next morning, the Fishermen caught in the meshes of their nets the body of the Woman with the little bound feet. But none would have guessed she had walked on such feet from the faraway Mountains. None would have guessed she had come to find her hero, that child of the Mountains, that brother of the Rocks, that friend of the Eagles, but instead found a Man always thinking of money, always dreaming of riches.

Oh, Magnificent River, enigma of the earth, mysterious Yangtze! Tell me, what have you done to the Youth of this country? What have you done to the Soul of this land? Are there not enough slaves in this world as it is? Are there not enough money-loving beasts on this Earth? Are there not enough covetous brutes in your cities? Oh, Magnificent River! Oh, enigma of the earth! Oh, mysterious Yangtze!

Chapter Fifteen

THE TRAGEDY OF THE CHICK

I

The other day a chick fell into the duck-pond and drowned. He was a strange little chick indeed. He never cared to play with the other little chicks, but always could be seen running about after the beautiful ducklings.

"I can't understand it," thought the Woman of the House. "Chicks should play with chicks, and ducklings should play with ducklings."

The chick grew terribly thin and weak.

"The poor thing!" cried the Woman. "I wonder if it's sick?" And she took him gently in her hands and looked him over. "But how does one treat a sick chick?" she asked herself after a pause. "It is hard enough to treat a sick human being."

She fed him some castor oil and pricked both his wings with a needle, but there was nothing she could do to cure him of his mysterious illness.

The chick grew weaker and weaker. Sometimes, when he leaned his head to one side, he looked like he was thinking.

"How does a chick think?" thought the Woman as she watched him. "It's hard enough to think as a human being." And for a time she was silent. "Oh, I should have known better," she murmured at last. "Besides, didn't I say before that chicks should play with chicks, and ducklings should play with ducklings?"

II

One day the little Chick was out playing with the Ducklings. It was late in the afternoon, and the sun was setting in the west.

"What is it you love most in the world?" said the Chick to the Ducklings.

"We love water," answered the Ducklings.

"Have you ever been in love?"

"No, we have not. But we have been in water."

"I see—And did you like it?"

"Yes, quite."

The sun was setting. The little Chick leaned his head to one side.

"What is it you think about when you swim in the pond?" he asked.

"We think about fish," answered the Ducklings.

"Is that all?"

"Yes, that is all."

"And what is it you think about when you play in the yard?"

"We think about swimming."

"Always?"

"Yes, always."

The sun had now set. The little Chick leaned his head farther to one side, until it drooped.

"Do you ever dream about chickens?" he asked.

"Never," answered the Ducklings. "But we dream about fish—big fish. In our dreams, they are bigger than the loaches that the Woman feeds us."

"I see," said the Chick, thoughtfully. "But who is it that you look for when first you wake up in the morning?"

"The woman who feeds us, of course," answered the Ducklings. "Don't you?"

"Well, actually . . ."

It was now evening-time. But the little Chick with the drooping head had not noticed.

"How I wish I could swim in the pond!" he sighed.

"In the pond!" cried the Ducklings. "But you don't even eat fish."

"Must I eat fish to swim in the pond?"

The Ducklings all looked at each other and shrugged.

As it was dark, the Woman of the House came out and called everyone in for the night, so the Ducklings and the Chicks left the yard.

Only the strange little Chick stayed behind, his head drooping before him.

"I can't understand it," said the Woman of the House as she watched him.

III

Early the next morning the little Chick was found dead in the duck-pond.

When the Ducklings saw this, they stuck their heads in the air and kicked their feet in the water. "How foolish!" they all said, and they nodded to each other knowingly. "He didn't know how to swim! And he doesn't eat fish, either."

Then the Woman of the House lifted the Chick out of the pond, and stared at his soaking-wet body. "The poor thing!" she said to herself at last. "If only he had known that chicks should play with chicks, and ducklings should play with ducklings . . ." And she continued to stare at the body of the little Chick for a long, long time.

And the sun began to set in the west.

Chapter Sixteen

FATHER TIME

I

Doubtless there is a large and bustling Beijing. My Beijing, however, is small and quiet. Doubtless there is a Beijing that is populated by great and noble men. My Beijing, however, is populated by honest and peaceful folk. Living in this quiet place, among these quiet people, my soul has begun to find some peace. But such peace has not been fully realized, and I fear that it never will.

My nights are terribly lonely. Alone in my bed I exert myself to sleep and dream. But while my Beijing sleeps very well indeed, I cannot sleep at all.

You see, my Beijing is not a place for dreaming beautiful dreams, but a place for forgetting those dreams that I once had many years ago.

When I think back to my days in Moscow and Tokyo, to those long sleepless nights when my friends and I would frequent plays and concerts and socialist gatherings, I cannot help but sigh. Huddled up under a single blanket with three or four friends, how we thought that we could save society, the nation—the whole human race even—from the clutches of rich and arrogant thieves; how we dreamed our dreams of a free world wrought by our own hands! Ah, when I think back to those times, I cannot help but cry.

At such times, I set a clock beside my head and try to hear in its ticking the familiar voices of my distant friends. (I am, after all, a poet, and can be expected to do such things.)

However, I have yet to hear anything in the ticking of the clock save for the harsh voice of Father Time, who, should he appear in one of his better moods, takes pity on me and speaks to me of many things—though what he tells me is never very happy . . .

Of late I have felt particularly lonely. To be sure, I believe that humanity is marching towards liberty, equality, and fraternity for all; and I pray night and day that our world might escape the persecution of those egoists who would trample on the rights of the vulnerable, and be delivered unto those who truly love mankind. But when I see how the youth continue to imitate their elders, beating their chests and repeating the same mistakes and crimes of their parents and grandparents, I begin to doubt the progress we have made.

Moreover, when I see how the youth continue to repeat the mistakes and crimes of their elders in all aspects of their lives, I fear that after many thousands of years of struggle, we have at last begun a pitiful retreat—a thought that makes me more lonely than anything . . .

The following tale was related to me one night as I lay in bed, trying to comfort myself with the naive thought that our youth would one day come together to correct the mistakes of their parents and grandparents, and atone for the crimes of their elders, and thereby clear the way for happier times.

Resigning myself to another sleepless night, I set the clock beside my head and tried to hear in its ticking the voices of my friends tirelessly working to deliver mankind from the persecution of rich and arrogant thieves.

But I heard nothing save the harsh voice of Father Time . . .

II

"Man is a fool . . . *Ticktock* . . . Always has been . . . *Ticktock* . . . Was a fool yesterday . . . is a fool today . . . will be a fool tomorrow . . . *Ticktock* . . . *Ticktock* . . .

"He won't evolve . . . *Ticktock* . . . Don't expect him to . . . *Ticktock* . . . Will beget fool after fool after fool . . . *Ticktock* . . . Will call it 'evolution' . . . *Ticktock* . . . *Ticktock* . . .

"And you pity him? *Ticktock* . . . There is nothing to pity . . . *Ticktock* . . . He hasn't been made a fool by others, but by himself . . . *Ticktock* . . . There is nothing to pity . . . *Ticktock* . . . *Ticktock* . . .

"Man is a fool . . . *Ticktock* . . . So were his parents and their parents before him . . . *Ticktock* . . . *Ticktock* . . .

"He thinks he must respect his elders, no matter how foolish they are . . . *Ticktock* . . . He can do as he pleases . . . *Ticktock* . . . Can worship his foolish ancestors for all I care! *Ticktock* . . . It's not like he won't turn out more foolish than they! *Ticktock* . . . *Ticktock* . . .

"Man is a fool . . . *Ticktock* . . . He will beget foolish children who will do foolish things and die fools themselves, having worshiped him and his foolish ancestors all their foolish lives. *Ticktock* . . . *Ticktock* . . .

"He thinks a new curriculum will save his children . . . *Ticktock* . . . What utter nonsense! *Ticktock* . . . What would that do? *Ticktock* . . . Teach them to speak English? Teach them to play billiards, baseball and football? Ridiculous! *Ticktock* . . . *Ticktock* . . ."

As I listened to Father Time, my eyes filled with tears.

III

"There once was a large old temple, unimaginably large and unimaginably old . . . *Ticktock* . . . *Ticktock* . . .

"And inside this large old temple were said to live many gods, all unimaginably large and unimaginably old—each with its own shape and color. *Ticktock* . . . *Ticktock* . . .

"And the elderly worshiped the gods, and performed many rituals before them, and the youth assisted them, spending all of their time protecting the gods and the temple, without giving the slightest thought to the lives that were passing them by. *Ticktock* . . . *Ticktock* . . .

"And among the precious offerings to the gods were man's sweat, blood and tears. But the most precious offering of all were the hearts and minds of the youth. *Ticktock* . . . *Ticktock* . . .

"And the main task of the young stewards of the temple was to prevent sunlight and fresh air from getting into the temple. *Ticktock . . . Ticktock . . .*

"For there was a prophecy that warned: were sunlight and air to enter into the temple, then all those who lived and worked in the temple would suffer the wrath of the old gods. And so the temple was always dark and dank, day in and day out. *Ticktock . . . Ticktock . . .*

"Lit by weak candles and shrouded in incense, the old gods appeared to be humongous, mystical giants. And the ritual for offering up the hearts and minds of the youth, which involved the intonation of a holy scripture full of hidden meaning, was an incredibly august affair. *Ticktock . . . Ticktock . . .*

"But due to the sacred music resounding in the heavy air, none could hear the cries of those who were being sacrificed— who wanted to live freely, who leveled curses at the gods. And due to the weak light of the candles and the smoke of the incense, none could see their sanguine tears, ghastly faces and spasmodic muscles made taut by suffering. *Ticktock . . . Ticktock . . .*

"And everyone believed that those who had been offered up to the gods were the happiest of men. Indeed, they never thought otherwise. *Ticktock . . . Ticktock . . .*

"That is, until a certain spring . . . *Ticktock . . . Ticktock . . .*

"And what a spring it was! For the sun shone brighter than it ever had before, and the air was clearer and mild. During that spring were the flowers more fragrant, did the birds sing more sweetly than the birds of previous springs. *Ticktock . . . Ticktock . . .*

"And holed up in the temple, the young stewards felt the spring more keenly than ever before, and longed for sunlight and fresh air. *Ticktock . . . Ticktock . . .*

"And one day the cries of those longing to live freely, those leveling curses at the gods, grew louder, so that everyone could hear them. And the sanguine tears, ghastly faces and spasmodic muscles made taut by suffering became more visible, so that everyone could see them. And for the first time did the young stewards suspect that their gods were mere sculptures brought to life by light and shadow. *Ticktock . . . Ticktock . . .*

"So they opened up a window, only an inch at first. *Ticktock . . .* And they saw that the sky was bluer than it had ever been before, and that the clouds were more beautiful. And their hearts yearned for truth. *Ticktock . . . Ticktock . . .*

"And lo! Lit by the light of the sun slipping through the slightly-open window, were the old gods revealed to be little more than stone sculptures. *Ticktock . . . Ticktock . . .*

"Paying no heed to the ancient prophecy that warned of the wrath of the gods to those who would let sunlight and air into the temple, the young stewards opened wide all the doors and windows of the temple at once. *Ticktock . . . Ticktock . . .*

"And as soon as the sunlight and the air were let into the temple did the old gods topple over the heads of the young stewards, and crush them. *Ticktock . . . Ticktock . . .*

"For the prophecy was not a lie. And all the young stewards who opened the doors and the windows of the temple were killed. But they were not sorry, even at the moment of their death. *Ticktock . . . Ticktock . . .*

"And even at the moment of their death did they look to the remaining youth who gathered round them, whom they had saved from the old gods, and said, 'Man will not be happy till the old gods are destroyed.' But under the influence of their newfound freedom, the remaining youth took one last look at the fallen gods and forgot about them entirely. *Ticktock* . . . *Ticktock* . . .

"And under the influence of their newfound freedom did some people begin to drink and gamble, while others obsessed over sports, and still others wrote and sang ballads. And at the height of their play did they forget not only about the old gods, but also about the young stewards who had died for their freedom, and their parting words. *Ticktock* . . . *Ticktock* . . .

"Meanwhile, the elderly, who were stunned but for a moment after the old gods came crashing down, could not forget at all. So they gathered together and raged angrily, saying, 'Let us rebuild the old gods, and close all the doors and the windows of the temple more tightly than ever before!' *Ticktock* . . . *Ticktock* . . .

"And cursing the sunlight and the fresh air, they repaired the broken gods and repainted them, and so restored them to their former state. And with the windows and doors closed once more, they dreamed of the day when they could resume their sacrificial rituals. *Ticktock* . . . *Ticktock* . . .

"But the youth who were under the influence of their newfound freedom noticed not a thing. And some of them drank and gambled, while others obsessed over sports, and still others wrote and sang ballads, oblivious to the fact that they would never be happy till the old gods were destroyed. *Ticktock* . . . *Ticktock* . . .

"*Ticktock . . . Ticktock . . .*

"Listen, the old gods are now nearly restored! And the sacrificial rituals are about to begin anew! . . ."

"Wait!" I cried out. "Father Time, please wait! You must tell me, what were those old gods you spoke of? And where was that old temple located?"

. . . Dong!

The clock chimed two . . .

IV

I got out of bed, my heart aching, my head spinning, my ears ringing with the cry, *Man will not be happy till the old gods are destroyed.*

"How I wish I could give my life for the happiness of mankind!" I groaned, and wandered despondently outside.

It was a cold November night in Beijing; a quiet Beijing night in November.

I grabbed the first person I came upon.

"Oh!" I exclaimed. "If only my heart were as cold as a November night in Beijing, and as quiet as a Beijing night in November!"

Chapter Seventeen

THE RED FLOWER

I

I was sleeping; and while I was sleeping, I was dreaming—I was dreaming of the fate of mankind, of the future of our planet . . .

My dreams were sad and lonely, dark and oppressive as our world. And yet I could not look away. I was dreaming after all.

There came a tapping at my window.

"Who's there?" I asked, and opened my eyes.

The tapping continued.

"It's me," came a voice. "The West Wind, harbinger of spring."

"Ugh! You had better not be that Wind of Beijing."

"I am the West Wind," the voice repeated, "harbinger of spring!"

"And what do you want?"

"To inform you that a new spring has arrived!"

"And what does that have to do with me? Look, I am busy dreaming about our planet. *'Spring has arrived'*—what nonsense!"

"But it's true! And it is more beautiful than anything you could ever dream of . . ."

"I don't believe you."

"And what's more, a new flower is coming into the world!"

"What kind of flower?"

"A Red Flower! A blood-red lily of the valley. Now, get out of bed and greet the new spring. A bird is singing of it, a beautiful bird."

"What kind of bird?"

"A Red Bird! A bright red swan—"

"If it is a swan, then surely it is singing its swan song, its song of death."

"Well, this swan is singing a blood-red song of life!"

"If you are going to tell lies, you had better make them good ones. Really, who ever heard of a blood-red song?"

"Have you never?"

"Certainly not. Now, would you please stop that incessant tapping? I am trying to sleep. I am trying to dream."

"No," said the West Wind. "I think that I will keep at it"; and he began to tap more forcefully at the window than before.

"Ugh! That nasty Wind of Beijing," I exclaimed, now wide awake. "He is always getting in somebody's way!"

II

Next there came a knocking at my door. *Ah, the boy has returned,* I thought. The boy was a sixteen-year-old student of mine who lived with me. I opened the door and, indeed, it was he. He rushed into the room without a word.

"What's wrong?" I asked him.

"The students are striking," he said after he had caught his breath. "There was a protest."

"Did it turn violent?"

"Yes," he said despondently. "We were beaten by the police and soldiers."

"Are you hurt?"

"No, not at all."

"I am glad to hear that."

There was a moment of silence.

"It wasn't only the police and soldiers beating us," the boy resumed. "When we got to the main road, ordinary people came out of the shops and restaurants and started beating us also. They jeered at us and called us names."

"Well!" I chuckled. "That must have been tough."

"Hey!"

The boy looked up in dismay, and then covered his face with his hands. *That was rather cruel of me*, I thought, and tried to apologize.

"Don't cry now. I was only joking."

The boy pulled down his hands. His lips were trembling.

"I'm sick of hearing jokes," he said. "Everywhere I go, I hear nothing but jokes. Must you tell them also? If you really felt sorry for me, you would talk to me about more serious things."

"Like what? Literature, perhaps? or Esperanto?"

"I don't mean that."

"Then what?"

He stared firmly at me.

"What is that look?" I demanded.

"I want you to tell me about the Red Flower," he said at last. The words came out so unexpectedly that I looked on him in wide-eyed amazement.

"The Red Flower?"

"Yes, the blood-red lily of the valley."

"And I suppose that you would like to hear about the bright Red Swan, too?"

This time it was the boy who looked amazed.

"What, is there really such a swan?"

"Yes, and it sings a blood-red song. Shall I sing it for you?"

The boy opened his mouth in awe.

I chuckled again, in spite of myself.

"Wait a minute," said the boy, his lips beginning to tremble again. "Is this another joke?"

"No, no, I promise."

"Everyone tells me that you have the Red Flower," he said, searchingly. "Is it true?"

"I am afraid not. And even if I did, it would be dead."

"Oh, yes," said the boy, looking down at the floor. "It would need light and warmth from the sun. But it will bloom," he exclaimed, looking back at me. "I can feel it!"

"How?"

"Because the sun is rising!"

I laughed, and there followed another brief moment of silence.

As if suddenly remembering something, the boy seized my hand.

"Give me the Red Flower. I don't mind if it's dead."

"What?"

"You know what I mean."

"Really, I don't."

"Then you must not love me," said the boy, smiling, and he let go of my hand.

I watched him walk over to the window. Leaning his tear-stained face against the glass, he stared out into the dark empire of night.

Somewhere a rooster could be heard crowing.

"The third crow . . . ," he murmured, fixing his gaze towards the east in eager anticipation of the coming sunrise.

I couldn't bear the sight.

"All right," I said at last, "I will tell you about the Red Flower. Only you must come away from the window."

"Why?"

"Because the sun will not rise."

"Not ever?"

"Perhaps not ever."

"But that was the third crow."

"It may have been the three-thousand-and-thirtieth crow for all we know. But come, do you really believe that a rooster can summon up the sun?"

"I suppose not . . . ," said the boy, and all at once, he began to cry, as a child might.

I tried to use every word of comfort in my vocabulary, but nothing could stop him from crying. So I lay his head on my lap and began to tell him the story of the Red Flower; and slowly but surely, he calmed down. Only the tears continued to fall from his eyes, and his body continued to tremble uncontrollably.

III

"This is a true story," I began. "It happened once upon a time.

"Long ago, in a certain kingdom, there lived a King and Queen whose names were Cold and Darkness. And they had two sons, Tyranny and Violence. The King's prime minister was a man called Larceny, and his most-trusted adviser was a sorcerer called Poverty.

"What the people of this kingdom suffered, my dear boy, you can never hope to imagine. Nor can a poor, inelegant speaker like myself ever hope to describe it. In short, their suffering was quite inexpressible.

"In the Kingdom of Darkness, there was no sun. So from the time the people got up in the morning to the time they went to bed at night, they would constantly lose their way in the streets, bumping into each other and falling into ditches.

"King Cold made sure that it was always winter, while Queen Darkness made sure that it was always night. Meanwhile, Tyranny and Violence ran about with their courtiers, howling the national anthem like mad dogs—

Hit them, hit them, make them fall
Strike them, strike them, kill them all!

"And as they ran about in this manner, they beat the men and molested the women and scared the children of the kingdom. Oh, my boy, you could hardly imagine such things!

"But that was not all, Larceny made incessant demands upon the people: 'Bring me your money!' 'Bring me your children!'

'Go over there!' 'Come over here!' he would shout. And Poverty would cast spells, so that the people trembled even in their sleep.

"Queen Darkness made the lighting of lanterns and lamps, even candles, a punishable offence; and King Cold decreed that anybody caught trying to warm their street or home would face a similar fate. Indeed, those who committed such 'crimes of convenience' came to the most fearful of ends . . ."

The boy looked up at me in wonder.

"What a terrible story!" he exclaimed.

"I assure you that it's not. And I know plenty of terrible stories. But this one really happened. It is not just a fairy-tale."

"What happened next?"

The West Wind was still tapping at my window, and a rooster was crowing for the three-thousandth-and-umpteenth time to announce the dawn . . .

"Although the kingdom was utterly impoverished," I went on, "the people held fast to a single hope. That is, like you, they waited for the Sun. This hope, and this hope alone, kept them going, generation after generation.

"For King Cold and Queen Darkness had promised them that if they waited patiently, they would relinquish the throne to the Sun as soon as it had risen, and live among the people as ordinary citizens. So the people saw it as their duty to wait for the Sun to rise, and indeed, they waited patiently. But no matter how patiently they waited, and no matter how many times the Sun rose and fell in other kingdoms, it did not rise in theirs. Meanwhile, the King and Queen bore another son, whom they named Despair.

"About this time, there arrived a foreigner by the name of Hope. He was a bright young scholar who knew many things. The only problem was that there was nothing the people in this land hated more than foreigners. Even the few foreigners who lived there hated them. And they hated Hope most of all because he spent all of his time pointing out what was wrong with their kingdom and planning revolutionary actions. 'The Sun will not rise,' he was alleged to have said; 'till the reign of Cold and Darkness is over.'

"But while the people had long lived in misery, most of them never doubted that their kingdom was the happiest kingdom in the world. So they paid Hope no heed. Only the hot-headed Youths displayed any concern, and they were the first to suspect that something might be rotten in the Kingdom of Darkness.

"When Tyranny and Violence heard this, they ran about with their courtiers, as was their wont, behaving more recklessly than ever, and howling the national anthem at the very top of their voices—

Hit them, hit them, make them fall
Strike them, strike them, kill them all!

"And, as was their wont, Larceny and Poverty swore their eternal allegiance to the Crown.

"Yet in spite of this, and after much debate, the hot-headed Youths went at last to seek out Hope and speak to him.

"'When will there be happiness in the Kingdom of Darkness?' they asked him.

"'When the Red Flower blooms,' he answered them plainly.

"And it just so happened that the kingdom was full of seeds of the Red Flower. So the hot-headed Youths immediately set about planting them, in schools and in temple gardens; in athletic centers and in parks; in one field and in another . . .

"Did the Red Flower bloom?" asked the boy.

"No," I said softly, "not one flower bloomed."

The boy let out a sigh.

Outside, a rooster announced the dawn for the three-thousandth-and-umpteenth time, while the West Wind continued to tap at my window, whispering: "It will bloom! The blood-red lily of the valley will bloom!"

But the boy could not hear them, he had once again buried his face in my lap.

"At any rate," I went on, "the hot-headed Youths sought out Hope for a second time.

" 'We planted the seeds of the Red Flower,' they said, 'but not one of them bloomed.'

" 'That is because they need light and warmth,' Hope answered.

"The Youths were thunderstruck.

" 'Then we have no choice but to wait for the Sun. After all, this is the land of Cold and Darkness. We can hardly expect there to be sufficient light and warmth.'

"There played a wry smile upon the lips of Hope. How sad that these people believed there was a Sun for every nation on earth, and that only theirs had not risen.

" 'Pardon my rudeness,' he said at length, 'but there is only one Sun, and it never stops shining. Only King Cold and Queen Darkness have prevented its light and warmth from reaching you. Which is why, were their reign to end, I believe that you would see the Sun. All that you need to do is get the Red Flower to bloom.'

"The faces of the Youths became dark and spiritless.

"'But you said it yourself: The Red Flower needs light and warmth.'

"And Hope laughed outright, and said: "The light and warmth needed for the Red Flower to bloom can be found anywhere on the earth.'

"The Youths all stared at Hope and wondered. And among them was a boy, much like you, whose name was Promise. Indeed, he was the most courageous and noble of all the Youths present. And taking up a knife in his hand, Promise cut open his chest and planted in his heart a seed of the Red Flower; and instantly there bloomed a blood-red lily of the valley.

"Soon there were Red Flowers all over the kingdom. And when they saw the blood-red blossoms, King Cold and Queen Hunger fled east, taking Tyranny, Violence, and Despair with them; while Larceny and Poverty fled west. After that, for the first time since the creation of the world, did the Sun cast its light and warmth on the Kingdom of Darkness, and the people came to know true happiness at last.

"But alas, young Promise, in whose lacerated chest bloomed the very first Red Flower, and many other young persons like him, was unable to see the brilliant shining sun over his homeland. For his lifeblood went into the lifeblood of the Red Flower.

"Now, my boy, surely you won't forget about Promise, and how he gave his life for the Red Flower to bloom . . ."

But the boy was asleep, his beautiful, weary head in my lap.

I looked down at him in silence. Somewhere outside a rooster was crowing for the three-thousandth-and-umpteenth time, while the West Wind continued to tap at my window.

The boy had begun to dream—and I also . . .

IV

I saw a crowd of laborers clamoring at the foot of a mountain, the peak of which was obscured by blue-tinted clouds. They were preparing to scale the narrow path leading all the way into the sky. Only along the path, from the foot of the mountain to the edge of the clouds, stood thousands of tax collectors, who refused to let the laborers pass. Suddenly, there leapt out of the crowd a young boy who proceeded to scale the path, handing out money to the tax collectors on either side of him as he went. The laborers watched him with envy till he disappeared behind the clouds. And when they could no longer see him, they began to clamor more loudly than before.

I went over to one of the laborers and spoke to him.

"What are you clamoring about?"

The laborer flashed me a suspicious look. "We came here to climb this mountain, but those bastards are asking for money," he said, pointing a finger at the tax collectors. "Why, we don't even have money for food!"

"Why do you want to climb the mountain?" I asked.

"Because we have been told that the Red Flower grows there, the Red Flower that will grant us happiness."

"And what is the name of this mountain?"

"Why, it is the Mountain of Learning, home of the Intelligentsia, the priests who created the flower that will grant us happiness! But we do not trust those scared little sheep, so we have determined to take the Red Flower ourselves. . . . The boy who went up was one of us. He promised to bring back the Red Flower. But then he had money, and we do not trust those with money. They are all thieves, the whole blood-sucking lot of them!"

At this, the laborers all shouted in one resounding voice.

"Hit them! Beat them!" They shouted as they began to march forward.

Suddenly, at the base of the blue-tinted clouds there appeared the recently departed boy.

"Ah, he has returned!" exclaimed the laborers, and they yelled out: "Hurry up! We haven't come to the mountain to play!"

So the boy hastened down the mountain, and each of the tax collectors hailed him as he went. Then, when he had come close enough for me to make out his features, I realized that he was, in fact, my student.

His eyes shone bright and his cheeks were red, and he called out to the laborers excitedly. But the laborers all looked at him in a daze, their mouths agape. I myself could hear him clearly, but was unable to understand what he was saying.

"What is he saying?" I said, turning to the laborer to whom I had been speaking previously. "I cannot understand him at all."

"I have no idea. That is no language of ours."

"What language could it be? The language of America, I wonder?"

"No, no—It is the language of the Intelligentsia. I believe they call it 'Academic.'"

Soon, the impatient howls of the laborers rose up one after another.

"Speak plainly!"

"Where is the Red Flower?"

"Give us the Red Flower!"

So the boy lifted the Red Flower up high.

"Here it is!" he cried.

And at once the crowd fell silent, so silent that I could distinctly make out the intense beating of their hopeful hearts. But after a minute had passed, there arose another cry that raged through the air like a storm at sea.

"That is a white flower!" they shouted. "A white paper flower dyed red! Indeed, you made it from parchment paper and red dye! You liar; you cheat! We will beat you!" And raising their clenched fists, they surrounded the boy.

"Stop!" I cried. "That is my student!" And I leapt into the crowd.

V

I came to my senses in a cold sweat, and glancing down, I saw that the boy was trembling in fear. I threw my neck back and closed my eyes, so as not to look at him, and placed my hand on his burning forehead.

"It was only a dream," I murmured. "None of it was real."

"I am not a liar," he sobbed, as if he were being interrogated by some unknown presence. "I swear it! I wasn't trying to deceive anybody. I really don't know how that paper flower got into my hands at all!"

"It was only a dream," I repeated, trying to comfort him. "None of it was real."

After a while, the boy calmed down and fell asleep again.

Then the door to my room creaked, and I had the distinct feeling that a new dream was about to begin.

"Don't come in here!" I wanted to shout.

But the boy had begun to dream—and I also . . .

VI

I saw a pyramid-like structure surrounded by an endless sea of people raising fearful cries. The steel gate of the pyramid was shut tight, so that not even the wind could pass through it. Machine guns and cannons stared down from a multitude of windows; and above and below stood an army of soldiers, cold as the stone of the pyramid, and hard as the steel of its gate. The soldiers stared unflinchingly at the sea of people before them.

"Open the gates!" cried the people, brandishing hammers, saws, pickaxes and other such working tools in the air. "Open the gates!"

The sea of people swelled. But the stone-cold soldiers did not so much as move one steel-hard muscle.

"Open the gates!"

I went over to a man who was brandishing an axe in the air, and spoke to him.

"What is this pyramid-like structure?" I asked.

"Why, it is Parliament!"

"Parliament?"

"Indeed, Parliament," he said, and resumed brandishing his axe and shouting, "Open the gates! Open the gates!" Then, turning to face me again, he went on angrily: "We have been told that the Red Flower is in there!"

"The Red Flower?"

"Indeed, the Red Flower that will grant us happiness."

"And the Red Bird?" I asked unthinkingly.

This time it was the man who wondered.

"The Red Bird?"

"Indeed. A bright red swan."

"Ah, perhaps it is in there also! We have just dispatched a representative to deliver us the Red Flower from the hands of the rich. But we never heard anything about a Red Bird. Surely the politicians have deceived us, those bastards! Ah, but what is taking our man so long? He should have returned by now. You cannot trust anybody who goes in there. They are all crooked bastards, every one of them, right down to the last atom!"

The cries of the people grew louder till, all of a sudden, a gate at the very top of the pyramid-like structure creaked open. Then the gates on all the other levels opened up, revealing a white marble staircase filled with perfect-looking flowers. On either side of the staircase were the most revered paintings and sculptures from every country in the world, and in between them stood a battalion of beautiful unmoving soldiers.

The sea of people froze as a boy appeared at the top of the staircase.

"Ah, that is our representative!" shouted the man next to me. "Isn't he fine!"

I looked closely and felt my heart leap.

"That is my student!" I exclaimed, putting my hand on his shoulder. "My friend!"

The man shook me off. "Liar!" he yelled.

The boy slowly descended the staircase to the growing cheers of the crowd, as behind him the steel gates closed one by one, till he had reached the bottom, and the pyramid-like structure had become, once again, cold, hard, and impenetrable.

"Where is the Red Flower?" groaned the sea of people. "Give us the Red Flower!"

By now I was certain that the boy was indeed my student.

The boy raised his hands augustly to reveal a blood-red flower to the crowd.

And once again, the sea of people froze, but only for a moment, for they soon began to shout and brandish their weapons in the air.

"That is a white flower! A white paper flower dyed red in the blood of the workers. A white paper flower dyed red in the blood of the poor! You spy! You murderer!"

"That is my student!" I cried. "That is my friend!" And I leapt into the crowd.

"Then you are to blame also!" yelled the man I had previously been talking to, and he rushed towards me with his axe.

I screamed and fell back, and a moment later felt his axe split my chest in two.

"My student!" I wailed. "My friend!"

VII

I came to my senses. I was trembling. Putting forth all my strength, I looked down at the boy whose head was still on my lap. His face was pale. Not a muscle was moving.

"Oh, god!" I exclaimed. "He's dead!"

I put my hand on his forehead. It was as cold. I looked at his chest and saw that it was split open. Then I reached inside and felt his heart. It was beating faintly.

I recalled that I too had been struck by an axe. Looking down, I saw that my chest was split open. I felt my heart. It was still beating, and inside it was a Red Flower, though mostly wilted.

"I have no need of this," I murmured, and plucking the Red Flower from my heart, I planted it in the heart of the boy.

His heartbeat picked up, and his formerly death-like face became full of life. But still a sad smile played about his lips.

"I am not a spy," he said softly, holding my hands tight. "I was really trying to bring back the Red Flower. I don't know how that paper flower got into my hands."

"Don't worry, my friend. I know. That was only a bad dream. None of it was real."

"I suppose so . . ."

The boy turned his face to the wall, and I turned that way also . . .

But the wall had disappeared . . .

VIII

I found myself in a square at the center of a city. To my left, I saw a mountain resembling the Mountain of Learning; to my right, I saw a building resembling the pyramid-shaped Parliament. The streets were swarming with people, all of whom were silent. In the center of the square was a stage, flanked by soldiers. Of the people I could see around me, most appeared to be farmers.

"What is that?" I asked a young farmer, pointing to the stage.

"Why, that is a scaffold," he answered plainly. "It is used for beheadings and hangings."

"Is someone to be executed today?"

"Indeed, someone is."

My heart winced.

"And who might that be?"

"Why should I know that? People get beheaded and hung here every day, but we don't know who they are or what they've done. But I'm sure there is a reason for it. Such people must have done something awful!" He looked round him anxiously, then continued in a low voice: "To be honest, I hear that they've beheaded people for nothing at all, or at least for some reason we ignorant folk wouldn't understand." And finally, coming right up to my ear, he said in a barely audible whisper: "We are only farmers apparently, not human beings."

I stared at him in shock.

"That is," he continued, "we are Shadows."

I felt my blood run cold. He really was a Shadow. I ran towards the scaffold. Fearing that the soldiers might be Shadows also,

I reached out and grabbed one by the hand. To my relief it was warm. The soldier turned his gaze on me.

"Tell me, who is to be executed here today?" I asked.

He grinned. "Why should I know that? People get beheaded and hung here every day, but we don't know who they are or what they've done. But I'm sure there is a reason for it. Such people must have done something awful!" He looked round anxiously like the farmer I had previously spoken to, and continued in a low voice: "To be honest, I hear that they've beheaded people for nothing at all, or at least for some reason we ignorant folk wouldn't understand." And finally, coming right up to my ear, like the young farmer had done, he said in a barely audible whisper: "We are only soldiers apparently, not human beings."

I stared at him in shock.

"That is," he continued, "we are Machines."

I shivered, and my blood ran cold.

I heard laughter behind me. Turning round, I saw a small crowd of people wearing red and black masks. They were laughing at me. I went over to them.

"Tell me who is to be executed here today?" I demanded of the red-masked people.

"Why should we know that?" they said, repeating word-for-word what the farmer and the soldier had said. "People get beheaded and hung here every day . . ." And they laughed, and the black-masked people laughed with them.

But I did not laugh.

"Who are you?" I asked.

"We are Masks."

"And where are your faces?"

"We have not yet received them."

"When will that be?"

"When the Red Flower blooms . . ."

"Tell me," I demanded again, "who is to be executed here today?"

"Why do you ask us this?"

"Because my heart pains me."

The Masks looked me over with suspicion.

"He is not a Shadow . . . ," they whispered to each other. "And he is not a Machine. . . . He appears to have a heart, and what's more, he says that it pains him."

Then one of the red-masked people stepped forward and said: "The person who is to be executed here today is the one who planted the Red Flower. It has been decided that he who sought to grant happiness to mankind should be executed."

"But who is he? And where did he plant the Red Flower? And where did it grow?"

"We do not know. We tried sowing it ourselves once, but in vain. No flower ever bloomed. That is why we have come here today."

All of a sudden, there arose a clamor. "He's here! He's here!" cried the Shadows and the Machines in one voice, and they formed two lines, between which drove an automobile draped in a black pall. As the automobile approached, an executioner holding a glinting axe ascended the scaffold.

The automobile stopped at the foot of the scaffold, and out of it stepped five or six soldiers and a highly decorated official. Together, they dragged out a young boy—it was he who was to be executed—and led him up the stairs of the scaffold. In the young boy's breast, I saw an immensely large Red Flower.

"That is my student!" I cried. "That is my friend!"

The soldiers lay the boy's head against the executioner's block, and the executioner raised his glinting axe into the air.

"Stop!" I shouted, leaping onto the scaffold. "You must stop! I beg you!"

The highly decorated official raised a hand, and the executioner held his axe firmly above my dear friend's neck. No Shadow nor Machine moved a muscle.

"Please," I implored. "The Red Flower is mine. If you must kill somebody, kill me."

The highly decorated official bent his little finger, and the executioner brought his axe down like a lightning bolt.

The boy's head fell to my feet.

"Oh, god! My dear little boy!"

IX

I buried my face in my hands and wept.

"Liar!" raved the boy. "The Red Flower is mine! I watered it with my own blood and warmth!"

"My dear boy, my dear little boy . . ."

The West Wind was tapping at the window more forcefully than ever.

"A new spring has arrived!" it continued to exclaim. "Won't you come out and greet it?"

The boy opened his eyes.

"Do you hear somebody at the window?" he asked, looking up at me.

I lifted my face out of my hands. "No, I don't think so."

"But I clearly heard somebody speaking."

"That is only the West Wind, harbinger of spring."

"Harbinger of spring?"

"Never mind . . ."

"But I swear that I heard somebody speaking. He said, 'A new spring has arrived. Won't you come out and greet it?'"

The boy stood up. The sun was now high in the sky.

"I have to go," he said.

"Where to?"

"Away. Won't you come with me?"

"I am on a different path."

The boy looked at me sadly. "I figured as much . . ."

"My boy, our paths may be different, but I am sure that they will cross again."

"At the scaffold, you mean?"

We went outside. The sky was clear and blue, and the sun was bright and warm.

The West Wind was shaking the leaves of a willow tree, and whispering: "Spring has arrived. Won't you come out and greet it?"

The boy took a deep breath and smiled.

"You know," he said as we were about to part ways, "I won't give it back."

"Won't give what back?"

"The Red Flower you gave to me."

X

In the garden, I bumped into the proprietress of the boardinghouse.

"Dear me!" she exclaimed when she saw me. "You look perfectly horrid! What in the world has happened to you?"

"Oh, nothing . . ."

"Did you have trouble sleeping again?"

"No, I slept quite well, thank you."

"Well, you really should go back to bed."

"You think so?"

"Yes, you look awful!"

The Willow Tree let out a sigh. "I think I will put forth some flowers," it said, "but not red flowers, I am afraid. That would be too much."

I stood in the garden for a long time, staring off into space.

APPENDIX

EASTER

TODAY IS EASTER SUNDAY. Last night I paid a visit to the Cathedral of Saint Nikolai, at Surugadai, with Akita and three other friends, to observe the evening mass. Akita said that he was very impressed. But I found it to be a poor imitation of the colorful Russian ritual, which remains in my memory a most wonderful affair, expanding my heart and filling it with joy whenever I think of it, wherever I may be. Was there really such a thing? No, there couldn't have been. It must have been a dream. Man often dreams . . .

Today, the house is empty. I am all alone. Outside it is raining. It has been raining since yesterday. Today is Easter Sunday.

Why does my heart hurt so much that I want to cry?

But I do not cry. My eyes are dry. And besides, I am not a child . . .

■ ■ ■

My family is dressed in beautiful clothing, in the largest room of my father's home.

"Christ has risen!" exclaims my father, and he kisses everyone present.

"Christ has risen!" exclaims my mother, and she kisses everyone; and my brothers and sisters rejoice and kiss each other in turn.

Then they all sit down at the table, on which is set some Paschal eggs and bread and other delicious foods. Between my father and my mother is an empty chair. Everyone looks at it as if waiting for someone to arrive. But no one arrives.

My father rises. "Vasya," he says to the chair. "Christ has risen."

■ ■ ■

I can hear him! Now somebody is sighing . . . No—It is no one. The house is empty. I am all alone. It is only the rain.

Why does my heart hurt so much that I want to cry?

But I do not cry. I have no tears. And besides, I am not a child . . .

■ ■ ■

I am celebrating with my family. But it seems like a dream. I am dreaming of when I lived in that small cottage in the lonesome countryside; when I lay beneath that apple tree, drunk on the sweet smell of apple-blossoms. One has pleasant dreams in the warm sun, with the murmur of a brook and the quiet hum of honeybees. Ah, how often man dreams . . .

Our village is surrounded by tall pine trees. Today my brothers and sisters will go and play there with their friends. It is tradition.

In the warm sun, the pines put forth their perfume. Everybody walks in twos, listening to the pleasant song of churchbells ringing like a choir in the sky. The youngest children are playing on a large swing in the field.

I hear the soft voice of Nina.

"Why has Vasya not come home for Easter?" she asks my elder sister.

■ ■ ■

Wait. What was that? Did somebody sigh? No—It is no one. The house is still empty. I am all alone. It is surely the rain.

Why does my heart hurt so much that I want to cry?

■ ■ ■

But I do not cry. I have no tears to cry. And besides, I am not a child . . .

I am playing among the pine trees with my brothers and sisters and our friends, when all of a sudden Nina takes me by my hand.

"They say that the blind are ugly," she tells me, laughing sweetly, "but I do not think so. For this morning when you kissed me for Easter, I had a good look at your face, and I saw how the others were wrong."

This memory—It seems to belong to one of the stories of Auntie Maria. All of her life she lived in a small clay hut.

Yet she told of the most wonderful palace of marble. She was poor and lived a hard life. But on cold winter days, she would sit with us children by the samovar and tell us about the happy lives of the royal family. At the time I wondered how she could know such splendid things. I wonder it still. She must have seen that marble palace, that happy royal family, in her dreams. Ah, how often man dreams . . .

■ ■ ■

My father is telling the family, as he does every Easter, how they must visit the graves of our grandparents and our other dead relatives. So they go to the graveyard, and kiss the crosses on top of the graves, saying, "Christ has risen! Christ has risen!" And they decorate the graves with flowers and place Paschal eggs on them.

Little Katya's grave is there.

I remember us crying, back when one of Roman's cows was dying from having eaten too much barley. To save its life, somebody had to cut its ear and let out the blood. Both Katya and I wanted to see the mystery. But our elder sister, Polya, went by herself, leaving us alone in the house. How mean of her, we said to each other.

Katya died when she was four years old. When she died, she suffered. She could not breath. She had diphtheria. Laying in the arms of my mother, she looked out the window, and waited for my father to return from the city.

"Mama?" she whispered. "What will Papa bring me as a present?"

Then: "Mama? Does Papa love someone more than he loves me?"

An hour after my father came home, she died. But when she died, she was smiling. For my father had brought her the most beautiful present, to let her know that he loved her more than anyone else in the world.

Indeed, Katya suffered. But she left this world smiling.

Why did she go to that other world? And for what? I still do not know. Since then, my father has always visited Katya's grave on Easter, where he says a few words in her memory.

I can see him there now, thinking, choosing his words. Everyone is gathered round him, waiting for him to speak.

"My Katya," he says slowly. "Vasya will not come home for Easter. He will never come home from that far-away land."

■ ■ ■

Somebody, somebody is crying. No—It is no one. The house is empty. It must be rain.

My god! When will it stop raining?

SOME PAGES FROM MY SCHOOL DAYS

I

I am blind, and have been since I was four years old, when, with bitter tears and grief, I left behind the realm of beautiful colors and brilliant sunlight. Whether my departure has been for good or ill, I cannot say for sure. What I can say, however, is that my night is a long one. Indeed, it will reign over me until my dying day.

Do I begrudge it? Certainly not. In his autobiography, *Hitting the Dark Trail*, the renowned blind author Clarence Hawkes has written: "The sun at noontide showed me the world and all its wonders, but the night has shown me the universe, the countless stars and illimitable space, the vastness and the wonder of all life. The perfect day only showed me man's world, but the night showed me God's universe. Though the night has brought me pain, and often discouragement, yet in it I have heard the stars sing together, and learned to know nature, and through nature to look up to nature's God."

Mr. Hawkes, for those unacquainted with the man, lost half his left leg as a child and was blinded at the age of fifteen—yet his stories of wildlife have made him one of the most famous natural scientists in America.

Can I say the same thing for myself? Perhaps had I lived like Mr. Hawkes, in a nice, warm cottage in a wood, surrounded by a large, loving family. But alas, though I long for Nature, I have had to live in the din of such great cities as Moscow, London and Tokyo.

In the din of these cities, the Night did not let me hear the stars sing together, nor did it teach me to know God by Nature. Rather, it taught me something else entirely, something that I shall not discuss now, for now I shall tell you about some things that were taught to me in school.

■ ■ ■

At the age of nine, I was sent to Moscow, to study at the Moscow School for the Blind. The school was entirely cut off from the world, a place where the students were at the mercy of their teachers. Nobody was allowed to leave it for any reason, not even to visit family during the holidays. In short, we were prisoners.

Once our teacher told us that the earth was so large that anybody could find a place to live on it if they wanted to.

"If the world is really so large," asked my friend Lapin, who was eleven years old, "why is it that my father cannot have a small piece of it to himself? And why is it that he must always rent the land of Count Orlov?"

Naturally, our teacher punished him for his "foolish" question. You see, in our class, we were only allowed to ask "smart" questions.

"Do you understand that your question was a foolish one?" asked our teacher after a time. But Lapin shook his head, so he had to stand in the corner until he did. It was only after having stood for half an hour that Lapin came to understand his folly and was allowed to sit down again.

After the lesson I asked Lapin how his question had been foolish.

He told me that he didn't know.

"But you said that you understood," I remarked.

"I understood that it is foolish to be punished for asking questions," was his reply.

Another time, our teacher told us that mankind was divided into several races—white, yellow, red, and black. The most civilized race, he said, was the white race, while the least civilized were the black and red races.

At this Lapin stood up. "Why?" he asked. "Is there something about being white that makes us more civilized?"

Another boy stood up. "And when the sun turns us dark in the summer, do we somehow become less civilized?"

The teacher dismissed both questions as foolish, and ordered Lapin and the other boy to stand in the corner until they understood their folly.

II

Our school was around the corner from the home of Sergei Perlov. Mr. Perlov owned the most well-known tea company in Russia and imported vast quantities of tea from China. Once, he invited the famous Chinese diplomat Li Hongzhang to his home. When Mr. Li found out that our school was around the corner, he eagerly requested a tour.

Mr. Li came to our school in a Chinese robe, with his hair neatly braided at the back of his head. He was very kind and let all the children touch his robe and hair.

Having heard that Mr. Li belonged to the "yellow" race, I grabbed his hand and tried to *feel* the difference of our colors. After several minutes, I turned to my teacher and asked: "Does Mr. Li really belong to the yellow race?"

The teacher assured me that he did.

"Then why can't I tell the difference between my white hand and his yellow one?"

To this, Lapin added: "If Mr. Li really belongs to the yellow race, he should be less civilized than us. But he seems to me to be much kinder than Old Mikhail."

Old Mikhail was the school groundskeeper, whom we hated for his meanness.

Mr. Li's interpreter whispered something to Mr. Li, and he laughed outright. Afterwards, Lapin and I were punished for being rude to our foreign guest. And we were not allowed to eat until we understood how rude we had been.

By the end of the day, we understood and were allowed to eat dinner with the others.

On the way to the dining hall, I whispered to Lapin that the hand of Mr. Li was nicer to touch than that of our white headmaster. Lapin whispered back that Mr. Li was not only kinder than Old Mikhail, but more civilized than all the white teachers in our school.

"What are you two whispering?" demanded our teacher as we entered the dining hall. "I want you to repeat what you just said now in front of everybody."

Unable to think up a lie on the spot, and stumbling over our words, we confessed. At this our teacher became very upset, and ordered us to kneel on the cold stone floor, saying that we were not to get up until we fully understood what we had done wrong.

Our stomachs growling, Lapin and I quickly understood what we had done wrong; and recalling every bad and baseless thing that we had been told about the Chinese from our teachers, and laying it all on the shoulders of poor Mr. Li, we said before everyone: "Li Hongzhang is less civilized and less intelligent than our white teachers, for he wears strange clothes, has ridiculous hair, and when he was small, wore little wooden shoes to keep his feet from growing bigger."

"Mr. Li didn't bind his feet!" cried one of our classmates. "That is only done by little Chinese girls."

"Doesn't matter!" said Lapin, bluntly. "If Li Hongzhang was a girl, he would have done so."

"What girl would bind her feet voluntarily?" cried another classmate. "It's the parents who make one do that."

"If he was his parent," responded Lapin, undeterred, "he would do it, I'm sure."

Everyone laughed, so we continued to invent ways in which Mr. Li was less civilized than ourselves: Li Hongzhang goes to public executions; he has ten wives; he loves his sons, but not his daughters; he drinks tea without sugar; he eats black cats for breakfast, white dogs for lunch, and rats dripped in honey for supper; when he comes across a louse, he puts it in his mouth and grinds it between his teeth . . ."

Several students began to look ill.

"Enough!" cried our teacher, throwing his spoon at us. We were pardoned and allowed to eat our supper. Everybody laughed—everybody except us. We only wept into our bowls.

"I said that you can eat," barked our teacher, "so why are you crying?"

But we made him no answer.

Seeing that we had not touched our food, he stormed over to us.

"What is the matter with you?" he demanded. "Why aren't you eating?"

"We are punishing ourselves," responded Lapin, "for having been so cruel and unjust to the good Mr. Li."

Our teacher said nothing.

That night I dreamed that I saw Mr. Li, with his fine silk robe and neatly braided hair. He was very kind, and his hands were pleasant to touch.

III

Our teacher once taught us that every land had a ruler, and that a land without a ruler was like a school without teachers—it simply could not progress.

We all smiled, for nothing made us happier than when our teachers fell ill, allowing us the freedom to amuse ourselves. Oh, what fun we had then!

Seeing our smiling faces, our teacher grew angry. "What's so funny?" he shouted. "Why are you all smiling? Smiling for no reason is a sign of guilt."

We said nothing.

"In Russia," our teacher went on, "we have a tsar who wears a costly crown on his head, and a costly cape on his shoulders. He sits on a throne, and holds a scepter in his hand . . ."

"What about when the Tsar isn't wearing his crown or cape; or when he isn't holding his scepter?" interrupted Lapin. "How should one know that he is the emperor?"

The question was a foolish one, and Lapin was made to stand in the corner. But he protested. "We never see his crown or cape!" he cried. "So how are we supposed to know?"

Indeed, the question was so foolish that he had to kneel on the floor.

"Aside from the Tsar," our teacher went on, "there are nobles. And we must always respect and obey the nobles, for they are of a higher class than ourselves."

Since Lapin was already on his knees, we had nobody to ask another foolish question, so a girl stood up, and said: "Langhov's father is a baron. Does that mean that we should show him more respect than our other classmates?"

Our teacher ordered her to stand in the corner.

"In our school," he went on, "we have fools like Lapin who are always trying to bother their teachers, just like how in Russia we have good-for-nothings who are always looking for ways to cause trouble for the Tsar. We call these people socialists, anarchists, and whatnot. You really should be afraid of such people."

But none of us were afraid of Lapin. We loved him more than any other student and thought that if the good-for-nothings of Russia were as friendly as this good-for-nothing of our school, we had no reason to be afraid of them at all.

Some time later, the Grand Duke Sergei Aleksandrovich, uncle to Tsar Nicholas II, paid a visit to our school. The grand duke was, at the time, the governor-general of Moscow. A week before his visit, we began making preparations at the school, learning how best to greet such a person of distinction.

Policemen and soldiers filled the school grounds, as well as the neighboring courtyards and streets. People were afraid that the anarchists or revolutionaries would attack the grand duke on his way to the school.

On the day fixed for the grand duke's visit, every preparation was made. We waited for the bell to indicate that it was time to gather in the assembly hall. Then, ten or twelve minutes before the scheduled time of his arrival, the bell began to ring. Thinking Old Mikhail was simply getting excited, I decided to wait a few minutes before leaving the dormitory.

On the way to the assembly hall, I was stopped by a strange man.

"Where are you going?" he asked me.

"To the assembly hall," I answered. "The Tsar's uncle is paying us a visit."

The man asked me if I had eaten breakfast.

I told him I had.

"Was it a good breakfast?"

"Why?" I asked. "Can you give me something better?"

"Certainly," answered the man.

"Then why don't you? The food here is awful."

He laughed. "Tell me, can you like a person you cannot see?"

"Of course I can. I cannot see my friends, but I like them very much."

"Do you like me?"

"I don't know you," I replied. "But even if I did, I probably wouldn't like you. At any rate, I don't have time to speak to you. The Tsar's uncle should be here any minute." And I headed towards the assembly hall.

I was later informed that during this conversation, the teachers had all turned white, then red, for the strange man who had stopped me was none other than the grand duke himself. With a royal wave of his hand, he had forbidden anyone from interrupting our conversation.

Afterwards, I was sent to the headmaster's office, where all the teachers gathered to discuss the possibility of expelling me.

"How dare you speak to the grand duke so rudely?" they shouted at me.

"But I didn't know it was him!"

"How could you not?" they demanded. "If you could not see his beautiful uniform, or the glittering badges on his chest, then at least you must have felt his majesty! Why, he was flanked by two towering Circassian guards; and behind him stood several lieutenants and adjutants. Really, even if you couldn't see them, you must have felt their presence."

"But I didn't feel anything!" I said. "I only thought that he was one of those nasty policemen patrolling our school and neighborhood."

After a while, the teachers saw that I had understood the gravity of my mistake and let me go. Back in the dormitory, Lapin told me that even had the grand duke worn a costly crown and carried a scepter in his hand, and was flanked by all the guards in Petrograd, he still wouldn't have believed that he was the grand duke, but would have fancied him some unceremoniously arrogant foot soldier.

IV

Earlier, I said that our school was entirely cut off from the world. That is not entirely true. Once every two weeks, our teacher, with the help of some school caretakers, would take us to the public sauna, which he rented out for two or three hours.

One day, on our way to the baths, Lapin and I slackened our pace until we were twenty or thirty feet behind the rest of our classmates. Always looking ahead, our teacher and the caretakers did not notice us go missing.

All of a sudden, we were stopped by a stranger.

"My dear boys," said a man's voice. "Where you are going?"

We quickly doffed our caps and saluted the stranger. "We are going to the public sauna," we responded politely.

The stranger laughed. "Why? Do you need to sweat something out?"

"Oh, yes," we answered. "Our teacher makes us go to the sauna every two weeks, that we might purify our bodies."

"And what about your spirits?"

"Our teacher never tells us to purify that."

He laughed again. "Did you not know that you should be purified as often as possible?"

"Oh, yes," we nodded. "In the rainy season, when we go out into the schoolyard, we always get dirty, for whatever we touch is dirty, and wherever we go, there is mud. But our teacher only punishes us then and does not take us to the sauna."

The stranger listened intently. "Nowadays it is always the rainy season," he said, sighing. "And no matter where we go, or what we touch, we are bound to get dirty."

But it was the end of August, and the weather was fair, there not having been any rain for two or three weeks, so Lapin and I naturally had some difficulty understanding the stranger's words.

We heard several men gather round us. Seeing our confused faces and mouths agape, they began to laugh. Just then, our teacher came running over, with two caretakers following close behind him.

"Naughty boys!" he cried, smacking both of our cheeks with the back of his hand. "How many times have I told you not to talk to beggars. Yet here you are, where the whole world can see you! Why, you are not even wearing your caps in front of these people, you incorrigible blind devils!" And he and the caretakers dragged us over to where the rest of our class was waiting.

At the sauna, our teacher called us to a separate room, where he took out a rod and said that he would punish us for having dishonored our school.

"What would the people of Moscow say," he cried, "were they to find out that our students talk to beggars in the street? What would they think about their teachers? Ugh! And that beggar! He was the most fearful thing I have ever seen in my life, what with his long nails, his dirty rags, his scraggly beard and unkempt hair. And those fleas that covered him whole, from his head to his bare, bloodied toes!"

The rod came down on my naked body. Then it struck Lapin, then me once more.

Clenching my teeth, I told myself that I would not cry or shed a tear.

"Please, sir!" cried Lapin, "we didn't know that he was a beggar!"

"Who did you think he was, then?"

"I thought," murmured Lapin, "I thought that maybe he was the duke . . ."

"With glittering badges on his breast!" I added.

We heard a sudden cry—one mixed with surprise and fear. Our teacher dropped his rod to the floor, and perhaps, for the first and last time in his life, saw, for a fleeting moment, our small realm of Night, with its duke of black fleas and glittering badges.

When Lapin and I returned to school, we expected more punishments, but our teacher did not so much as speak to us. I imagine that he was afraid to speak even to the headmaster about what had happened. After all, it was due to his negligence that we had spoken to the beggar, and, of course, he did not want to be punished either.

■ ■ ■

Before I conclude this brief sketch, I should like to say that if the Night has taught me anything, it has taught me to doubt everything and everyone; to suspect the words of teachers as well as the slogans of authority.

So now I doubt everything and suspect all forms of authority. Indeed, I doubt the goodness of God as much as I do the evilness of the devil; and I am as distrustful of governments as I am of those who put their faith in them.

To be sure, the Night has taught some blind people to keep quiet. Most of my friends have come to accept everything that was said by our teachers as true, and now believe every word that is handed down to them by the authorities. They doubt nothing, and so have been able to make a place for themselves in society as musicians, teachers, and laborers . . . They live comfortable lives, these friends of mine, surrounded by loving families, while I have been able to make no such place for myself, doubting everything and everyone as I wander from one land to the next.

Ah! But who can say that one fateful day I will not be standing at the darkened corner of some noisy street, like that Duke of the Night, extending my hands and begging to everyone who passes me by?

MY EXPULSION FROM JAPAN

JUNE 4, 1921—That was the last day of my life in Japan. I prayed that it would be the last day of my life here on earth, but no god, it would seem, cared to listen.

After receiving my deportation order, I was escorted by a cordon of police officers to the *Hozan Maru*, a large steamship bound for Vladivostok. Only two people came to see me off—one a newspaperman from the *Asahi Shimbun*, the other a business school instructor who occasionally served as a Russian interpreter for the Tsuruga Police Department. Sympathetic to my plight, they kindly stayed with me until my ship set sail. Whenever I tried to speak to them, they cautioned me with anxious looks, and said: "Don't speak! The police are listening." So I kept silent. But even in my silence, I am certain that they understood something of the infinite sorrow and indescribable loneliness that I was feeling in those moments.

I was expecting some friends from Tokyo to see me off. But nobody came.

Or nobody could.

The newspaperman and the Russian interpreter accompanied me to the steerage level, where they stowed my bags and helped me to find my cot.

Then, under the watchful gaze of my escorts, Lieutenant Akahoshi and Detective Nakayama, we returned to the deck.

But no matter how long I waited, nobody from Tokyo arrived.

A gong sounded, indicating that it was time for my companions to go. The newspaperman and the interpreter each gave me one last firm handshake in which I felt the warmth of my dear friends back in Tokyo. Then they alighted from the ship.

There was another, louder gong, and the three-thousand-ton *Hozan Maru* boldly made haste towards the open sea. Needless to say, I was in no mood to do the same. Not yet prepared to set out upon the open sea of life, I leaned against the cold, hard railing of the ship and continued to wait for some friend, any friend, to call out my name. But nobody was coming. Or nobody could. Or perhaps they thought that it wasn't necessary.

I did not cry.

Japan had once seemed to me to be a faraway place. Now it was more dear to me than Russia. And I was leaving it forever, expelled without having said goodbye to those who had become more dear to me than family.

I did not cry—only my voice grew hoarse, and my throat dry, till I became dizzy and nauseous. I had one of the escorting officers take me to my cot. My head and my heart felt empty, as if I were growing more and more distant from my soul.

It was not yet five in the afternoon, but I was suffering, so I tried to sleep. Whether I fainted or not, I am not sure, but as I was beginning to lose consciousness, I distinctly remember praying that I would not wake up.

■ ■ ■

Many of the first- and second-class passengers on board were men and women who had fled to Japan from Tsarist Russia to escape the Bolsheviki. Now that the Bolsheviki had lost control of Vladivostok, they were making their triumphant return.

In the steerage, the situation was different. There, a group of over twenty laborers were returning from America to Soviet Russia, their new "land of opportunity."

To the Japanese, the word "Soviet Russia" surely conjures up fearful images of some hellish place, or worse. But to the Russian laborer toiling in America, it represents nothing short of Paradise restored. And so tens of thousands of laborers were now throwing away everything that they had worked for in America for a chance to return home.

The laborers in the steerage were one such group. Among their party were six children and an elderly couple, the Katkovs. Naturally, the children spoke no Russian. But to my surprise, even the laborers had forgotten it. In fact, I did not come across one single person among them who could speak the language with fluency.

All of them had been born in Russia, where they had learned their love of Freedom under the oppressive Tsarist regime of Nicholas II. Unable to bear the terrible yoke of tyranny, these poor, peasant folk sought Freedom across the sea, in that strange, faraway country called America. And it was in America that they found it—but it was not free, for in America, Freedom comes at the cost of one's heart and soul.

Once in America, those who would barter away everything became living machines. Machines operating other machines—such is the Freedom of the American business world. Meanwhile, those unwilling to sell their souls—that is, unwilling to become mere cogs in America's inimitable society of living machines—had no other choice but to become anarchists or take up membership with the IWW.[1] Hoping to disrupt the factory of American society, they shoved sticks into its gears and hurled rocks into its springs. Despising the world, and being despised in return, they came to eke out a strange existence.

These were men and women who had seen the inside of American jails more than once. Some had even done as much as five or six years. And all of them were either anarchists or card-carrying IWW members. That said, not one of them was a deportee—which perhaps explains their surprise when they saw me being brought onboard against my will. Who could he be, they must have wondered, and what on earth did he do?

I awoke from a strange dream to find a crowd of people at my side. They were speaking about me in hushed tones.

"I'll bet that he tried to start an anarchist club in Japan."

"Oh, he is an agitator no doubt."

"I imagine that he had some hand in the Revolution."

---

[1] Translator's note: *IWW*, Industrial Workers of the World.

I sat up in my cot.

"Well?" asked the crowd in one voice, as though they had been waiting for me to get up for some time. "Why did they deport you? You must have done something awful."

"Actually, I didn't do anything at all," I answered. "It was the people who deported me who did something awful."

Pegging me for some kind of noble troublemaker, the laborers urged me not to be so modest and tell them what had really happened.

Not knowing what to say, I began to tell them about my life in Japan—about the socialist friends I had made there and my participation at socialist meetings; about the children's stories that I had published and the recitals of Russian folksongs that I had given; and how for all that was I deported from the country. My captive audience felt sorry for me, and their already ill-feelings towards Japan grew a hundred-fold.

■ ■ ■

At meal times the laborers spoke bitterly of the steamship company. They threw plates, spilled soup and bothered the waitstaff, who complained to the ship's crew, saying they simply could not deal with such "radicals." The laborers were demanding unconditional Freedom, and in their eyes, the steamship company represented Tyranny itself.

Freedom—it was all that these people spoke or dreamed about. And when the gray reality of their lives ran counter to their rose-colored dreams, they drank and sang as a form of escapism. But what exactly was this Freedom that they pursued?

Not even they themselves knew for sure. To them it was perfect, shapeless, and utterly undefinable.

In the steerage, aside from the laborers, were a few Russian university students returning from Hong Kong. Supporters of the Kerensky administration, they often got into fierce arguments with the laborers. And whenever the laborers became vexed by their overly logical thinking, they would come to me to hear songs of Freedom. Although at the time I would have rather sang songs of mourning, I would nevertheless take up my balalaika and indulge them. These songs always seemed to give them courage. Then, with hearts reignited, they would drink and continue arguing with the students for hours on end.

The voyage to Vladivostok only lasted two days and one night, but that was enough time for me to befriend these hard-working men and women of the earth.

The Katkovs doted on me as if I were their child. Chizhinsky, the young and charismatic leader of the group, treated me like a brother. And the others looked up to me with an undue reverence that made me blush.

■ ■ ■

On the morning of the sixth, at about eight o'clock, somebody shouted that they could see Vladivostok, and everybody rushed out on deck to look. Some were gushing with joy while others were hanging their heads anxiously.

From the stern of the ship, the laborers gazed on Vladivostok, the birthplace of the new Russia's sorrow and rage.

While I stood among them, my body and soul were turned eastwards, towards Japan.

Suddenly, everybody fell silent. Their silence expressed better than words the terrible unease that they were feeling. Chizhinsky held my hand. His own was as cold as ice.

"What's wrong? Are you cold?"

"No . . . It's just that I was hoping to see the red flag over Vladivostok."

I felt a hot teardrop fall on my hand.

"Ah!" I started, surprised by the heat of Chizhinsky's tears.

"Are you all right, Vasily?"

Everybody turned round and looked at me.

"No, no, it's nothing," I murmured, turning my face yet again eastward.

"Chizhinsky," I said after a pause. "If the red flag is not flying over Vladivostok today, then you should work to make it so tomorrow."

"Indeed. No matter what the Japanese or any other empire says, we will fly it."

Chizhinsky's grip tightened as he spoke, but his hand remained ice-cold. I felt another burning teardrop fall on my hand.

Beside me, Mikhail, an anarchist and the scion of a wealthy family of the imperial era, began to sing a revolutionary song—

Comrades, let us join
Our strong hands against tyranny
To build ourselves
A free world on earth . . .

"Careful," I remarked. "Someone might hear you."

"So what?" cried Mikhail, angrily. "Let them try to stop me. We anarchists are not afraid, not like these cowardly Bolsheviki here!" he added mockingly, referring to the Leninist laborers who were in our group.

There was some nervous laughter, but nobody was in the mood for humor.

"Comrades," I exclaimed, "you should be ashamed of yourselves. How will you behave when real tragedy strikes?"

"Speak for yourself," said Mrs. Katkov. "You are just as pale as we are. And what's more, your eyes are wet, and your lips are trembling . . ."

"Not because I can't see the red flag," I answered.

"Don't tell me that you still long for that damned Japan!" reprimanded Chizhinsky.

I smiled weakly, but gave no answer. I did not want to admit that the more space put between me and "that damned Japan," the more dear it became.

From the second-class deck came the cheers of Russian soldiers.

"Ah, Vladivostok has been restored! Gone is that awful red rag, and in its place flies our beloved tricolor! Hurrah!"

"Soldiers!" cried their lieutenant, "Russia shall be restored to its former glory! Let this be her first step towards true Freedom!"

"Freedom!" echoed the soldiers.

But we on the steerage deck said nothing.

"Look over yonder!" the lieutenant continued. "That there is our dear father Ataman Semyonov's ship, where the Russian and Japanese flags fly together in a cross that will one day fly over all the nations of the world! May God protect us and our Japanese brethren as we march hand in hand into battle!" And removing his cap, he made the sign of the cross. And the other soldiers did the same. "May God protect us and our Japanese brethren as we march forward—to Moscow! To Petrograd!"

The laborers from America all hung down their heads. Chizhinsky leaned against my shoulder and wept like a child.

"Oh, Vasily," he sobbed, "say something, won't you? Comfort us poor laborers who have abandoned everything in America."

His words moved me. "My brother, Chizhinsky," I said, putting my hand on his shoulder. "Why is it that you weep? For want of a red flag? Well, there is plenty of cloth to sew one from! Mind you the red flag is not a toy. No, you can leave those for the Japanese socialists to play with. Besides, you heard what the lieutenant said about those flags and the cross that they form. Well, just as Christ was crucified on a cross for bringing new ideas into the world, so does General Semyonov and his men intend to crucify the new Russia. Ah, but the new Russia is not the Christ who was crucified, died, and was buried. No, she is the Christ reborn! And those who cannot see this are among the Pharisees. Soon the flags of General Semyonov will only fly above the graves of his followers. Do you understand me? If you want to see the red flag fly over Vladivostok, you will have to raise it with your own sweat and blood!"

"Fear not," responded Chizhinsky, comforting me in turn. "We will."

■ ■ ■

A short time later, a quarantine launch carrying officials from the Vladivostok government pulled up beside the *Hozan Maru*.

"Ready your documents and gather on the first-class deck," shouted one of the waitstaff, and everybody began shuffling upstairs.

I was about to head up myself when Chizhinsky stopped me.

"If they lay a finger on you . . . ," he began to say.

"Don't worry," I said smiling. "I'll be all right."

Upstairs, the immigration officer checked the tickets of the first- and second-class passengers. Then, as he was moving on to the third-class passengers, there entered a Japanese official who spoke to him about me in Russian. He spoke in such a low voice that I had some trouble making out exactly what he was saying. Only the surprised responses of the immigration officer reached my ears.

". . . Eroshenko? . . . I see . . . Very well . . . We will have to be careful then, won't we? . . . Don't worry, I won't let him out of my sight . . ."

After the Japanese officer left, the immigration officer turned to me and spoke.

"Why were you deported from Japan?" he enquired.

"Why don't you ask my escorts?" I answered.

"I was told that you are a socialist. Are you one of the Bolsheviki?"

"I am interested in them."

"Well, I have been told many things about you. But not to worry. Our government is not in the business of bullying people, especially the blind. So if you want to go to Soviet Russia, you may go. And if you want to stay in Vladivostok, you may stay for as long as you like."

He let me go without charging me any duties.

When at last I disembarked from the ship, I was met by some representatives of the Vladivostok Esperanto Association.

Lieutenant Akahoshi and Detective Nakayama carried my luggage for me. "You are a free man now," said the lieutenant, warmly. "Let us shake hands."

So we did.

And with that I bid farewell to my beloved Japan forever.

■ ■ ■

The tricolor flag was flying over Vladivostok. Beneath it gathered all those who were antagonistic to, or antagonized by, Soviet Russia—that is, the nobles, priests, capitalists, and the intelligentsia. It was to Vladivostok that Semyonov and Kappel had retreated after having shed much blood across Siberia, from the Urals to the Sea of Japan. And it was from Vladivostok that they were preparing to make their last stand. Having nowhere left to retreat to, the Semyonov and Kappel armies were fighting for their very survival, and willing to give their lives for the supreme leader of the antirevolutionary forces, Admiral Kolchak.

In Vladivostok, the tricolor decorated not only roofs and windows, but also hats and lapels, and was reflected in every word and action on the streets of the city. It did not matter whether one was White (anti-Soviet) or Red (pro-Soviet), one wore the tricolor flag to hide one's *true* color, as it were. Should the

Whites be defeated, the people of Vladivostok would probably cheer and dance about in the streets; and should the Reds be defeated, they would probably drink and be merry all the same. But such people are the by-product of a new decadence. Indeed, you would be hard pressed to find their kind elsewhere.

The city's local Esperantists gave me a royal welcome. They had heard of me and were upset to learn that one of their own had been expelled from Japan. They promised to inform the international Esperanto community about Japan's abuse of power.

The chairman of the association, Mr. Vonago, urged me to stay with him until the situation settled down. In order to dissuade me from moving west, he read to me articles from the *Vladivostok Bulletin* (a Russian-language Japanese newspaper).

Included among the headlines were:

—White Army Wins Yet Another Victory! Reds Forced to Retreat

—Khabarovsk falls! Chita Ready to Capitulate

—Lenin Assassinated! Trotsky Smuggled from Russia by Actress-Lover

—General Semyonov to March on Moscow!

For Japanese journalists in the Far East, writing such articles had become a divine mission and was looked on as an act of patriotism. But there were far more idiots writing them than there were idiots who believed them.

Desperate to break free from this tricolor town, I began packing my bags immediately. There were a ridiculous number of things to consider. Although my belongings primarily consisted of simple necessities—bread, canned goods, sugar, tea, dried salmon, matches, soap, thread, needles, and the like—I felt as if I were setting out on some perilous journey.

There was a young female student named Tosya boarding at the chairman's house. Her native village of Povarovka was located on the Ussuri River, near the Russo-Japanese border, which I needed to cross. We quickly became friends. When she asked me to accompany her to Ussuri, I had the excuse that I needed to go. Her father was a doctor in Vladivostok, and her stepmother worked as a midwife. Neither of them opposed to her going. In fact, her stepmother promised to come to Povarovka soon after us.

■ ■ ■

On the morning of June 11, Tosya and I left Vladivostok.

Sharing the train car with us were a handful of Kappellite soldiers, two Semyonov officers, a priest and three gentlemen of the intelligentsia. Initially we all spoke of banal tricolor topics, with not a little unease; but after some time had passed, we came to know each other more on more intimate terms.

When the Semyonov officers learned that I had just arrived from Japan, they asked me to tell them what the Japanese thought of their great leader, not because they themselves wanted to know, but because they wanted others to hear. Seeing as I had lived in Japan for some time, they thought that I would offer up some fine words of praise.

However, being as I am of a nature that hates to pay compliments to soldiers, I did not at all hide my disdain for the man.

"Most Japanese think Semyonov a foolish pawn. Even the Russians there call the Ataman a traitor for taking money from Japan."

"Hold your tongue!" shouted the officers, angrily, but the Kappellite soldiers and Tosya managed to calm them. Meanwhile, the gentlemen laughed, and the priest muttered to himself, "Blessed is the man that walketh not in the counsel of the ungodly . . ."

Observing these representatives of Kappel and Semyonov closely, I found the former to be somewhat more civilized than the latter. Although I did not observe them for very long, I am sure that I would be able to distinguish them by voice alone.

One of the Semyonov officers downed two or three shots of vodka to calm his nerves.

"Goddamnit!" he started up again, slapping his thigh. "Who do you expect us to take money from? We are fighting in the Far East, are we not? Therefore we are not betraying Russia. We are trying to save her. And Japan is not using us. On the contrary, it is we who are using Japan! Ataman Semyonov will lead us to Freedom, to happiness. And those who cannot see that are our enemies. But wait—you aren't a Bolshevik, are you?"

Tosya squeezed my hand as if to tell me to keep quiet.

The priest continued to mutter to himself: "The Lord is my shepherd; I shall not want. He maketh me to lie down in green pastures: he leadeth me beside the still waters . . ."

The gentlemen smirked to one another.

Then the officer shoved a glass into my hand.

"Drink up," he exclaimed in a more affable voice. "To Russia!"

"I don't want to."

"Ah-hah!" he laughed, patting me on the shoulder. "So you're a communist! No matter, no matter. Come on now, drink. Nobody is watching anyways." And turning to the priest, he added: "How about it, Father? Care for a drink?"

Fearing that he would be labelled a communist if he did not comply, the priest downed three glasses of vodka. The Kappellite soldiers did too.

The more the priest drank, the freer his speech became, till he began to preach to us, and to me in particular, as if for his upcoming sermon in Nikolsk.

"So you think communism some perfect thing come down from heaven, eh? And Lenin, the new prophet, eh? Very well. I can certainly see why. For after the Kerensky administration fell, Petrograd was so enveloped in smoke that it seemed to be Mount Sinai itself. And Lenin appeared like the Almighty, who with thunder and lightning handed down his commandments to the Jews. Oh, but your Sinai has been replaced by a Golgotha, and your Almighty, Lenin, has revealed himself to be the devil. And now there hangs an innocent Christ from the cross on the Golgotha that you yourselves have . . ." And the priest trailed off, the image of Russia as Golgotha having brought him to the verge of tears.

"Pray, good Father, who is the Christ that Lenin has crucified?" asked one of the gentlemen from Vladivostok.

"Why, it is the Russian Church!" wailed the priest. "So we must bless Ataman Semyonov and our Japanese brethren, for sending us soldiers to deliver our innocent Christ from the hands of the infernal devil Lenin!"

I was about to respond when a man who until then had been sitting silent some seats ahead of us stood up. He wore a tricolor flag on his hat.

"What, you think that foreigners will save your Christ? Bah! Christ was his own savior, was he not? He needs no other. Indeed, your Russian Church is nothing but a den of thieves and cheats! No, it really deserves to be crucified!"

The priest looked away, drawing up his shoulders in embarrassment. I was shocked. "Ah, now we are getting somewhere!" snickered the gentlemen from Vladivostok.

"You who beg at the door of the foreigners," the man railed on, "you are of the Pharisees! You see the blade of Cain in the olive branch of Gabriel. You make the kiss of Judas a greeting among your brothers. You are blind and deaf! You couldn't see or hear if you wanted to. Indeed, you are of the Pharisees, I tell you! You should be on your knees, day and night, praying, 'Have mercy upon me, O God, according to thy lovingkindness. For I acknowledge my transgressions: and my sin is ever before me—' Well? Admit it!"

The train let out a whistle and came to a stop. Then the man gathered up his things and walked briskly to the end of the car.

The gentlemen from Vladivostok burst out laughing.

■ ■ ■

Our train went as far as Evgenievka, four or five stops from Nikolsk, where the Kappellite forces were centered. From there to the Ussuri River extended a sort of neutral zone held by the Japanese interventionists.

Of course, this so-called neutral zone was filled with danger and occupied chiefly by partisans and bandits who did as they pleased, ambushing the Reds and warring with the Whites, raiding villages, and causing all sorts of trouble for the Japanese. Who knows why the Japanese even stayed—to hold back these partisans and bandits, or for some other purpose? At any rate, they were apparently suffering from a lack of manpower . . .

As there were no regular trains running from Evgenievka, we had to continue our journey by armored train, the windows of which were filled with sacks of sand and gravel. In our dusty compartment were two middle-school students. When Tosya and I entered, we all agreed to open our window, to let some light in, saying to ourselves how exciting it would be if our train were to get attacked by bandits. Ah, but neither bandits nor partisans showed up, and after five or six hours we arrived safely at Ussuri Station.

How boring!

Ussuri Station was the last stop in the Japanese-occupied neutral zone before the country at last opened up into Red territory. The waters of the Ussuri flowed busily between a world we knew well and a new world of red flags, crimson clouds, and black smoke. These were two worlds connected by a single, half-destroyed bridge. When we arrived, the Red Army was just laying down explosives to blow the bridge to smithereens. Unable to come to an agreement with the Japanese, they saw no other option. In town, a rumor was spreading about Semyonov's army advancing on the Ussuri River.

Aside from a few cars bringing Red officers and state dignitaries back from Vladivostok, there were no trains departing from Ussuri. Ordinary travelers loitered about the station, heaping curses on the communists. Sometimes somebody would grab hold of the commissar and demand information on the next departing train. Despite being but eighteen years of age, he was full of arrogance and refused to indulge anyone.

Feeling sorry for these stranded travelers, the Japanese asked the Reds to send a train for them, but it was no use. So long as you were not a communist or a dignitary, you simply were not getting on a train. Everybody was terribly vexed.

■ ■ ■

I decided to put up at Tosya's family home until Fate was prepared to have me move on. Tosya's stepmother arrived a day later.

I had not been in the Russian countryside in years!

Tosya's home had a small yard with a vegetable garden in it. Each morning we would get up to water the plants and vegetables, and when the sun was high, we would go for a swim in the Ussuri River. Later, when we were tired, we would sit in the shade of a tree and read. In the evenings, we would walk about in the garden. And at night we would sit with her stepmother by the samovar, holding debates and singing songs. You would hardly know there was a war going on. It was such a carefree life, and I had a lot of fun.

In Ussuri, I made friends with two village school teachers and the parish priest, as well as several students from the local seminary, who earned their living working just as hard as the farmers did.

The people of the village had moved to the region some decades ago, and after many trials and tribulations had carved out for themselves a fairly comfortable life. Needless to say, they all despised the communists.

I had been told many times before how the farmers hated the communists, but until then, I had never been able to understand why. That the capitalists, who had lost great sums of money and position, hated the communists was obvious. But the farmers? They had no money or position to lose. In fact, they only stood to gain from the communists. And so I assumed that their hatred was borne out of pure ignorance.

However, after arriving in Ussuri, I came see that to lose what one had earned with one's own sweat and blood, even if it only amounted to a few dozen kopeks, was a far greater loss than to lose millions that one had earned through stock-market trading and exploitative labor. "It is easier for a camel to go through the eye of a needle," said Christ, "than for a rich man to enter into the kingdom of God." I wonder if the farmer clinging to his meager possessions has as much difficulty? Surely, these farmers would serve whomever, be they Russian or Japanese, should they be allowed to keep their possessions for themselves.

■ ■ ■

Everybody in Ussuri tried to dissuade me from crossing into Soviet Russia. And the village life was so carefree and delightful that I actually considered staying for the rest of the summer. Tosya invited me to her parents' apiary some twenty versts away.

And the parish priest suggested that I put up for a few months at the seminary in Simakov.

But just as I was about to make my decision, there arrived from Vladivostok the party of laborers from America who had been with me on the *Hozan Maru.*

These laborers, who had just experienced the utter incompetence of the Merkulov administration, seemed completely changed. After having been robbed by customs officials and cheated by some rogue who claimed to be a communist official from Chita, they had become dispirited, and were understandably in a great hurry to enter Soviet Russia. Nothing could persuade them to stay a minute longer.

However, the sight of me brought a smile to their weary faces—the first smile they had worn since landing in Vladivostok—and they were desperate to get me to come with them. So I scrapped my plan to spend the summer in the country. Naturally, my new friends in Ussuri begged me to reconsider, but I had firmly made up my mind to leave.

Since the arrogant and incompetent communists were still unwilling to resume ordinary railway services, the laborers and I decided to rent a few wagons, in which we would store our luggage, and set out for Iman. Arrangements were made for myself and the Katkovs to ride in a Red Army ration car, while the rest were to follow the wagons on foot.

Finally, on the evening of June 22, I said goodbye to my friends in Ussuri, and arrived safely in Iman the next morning. When the laborers arrived at six that evening, they were tired—tired, but happy to know that they were closer to Soviet Russia, for they believed that all they needed to do was cross the border and they would find their happiness waiting for them. Not one of them suspected that our journey would end up a miserable failure.

For, you see, I was ultimately denied entry into Soviet Russia. And while the laborers crossed over in sheer ecstasy, they were soon sent off to the dark mines of the north. In the blink of an eye, our journey was over.

Harbin, China

CHUKCHI PASTORAL

A CHUKCHI STORY

The great sea sleeps in the midday sun; and I sleep next to it on the seashore. The great sea dreams, and I dream its dream.

It dreams of a boat: no mast, no oars, no rudder; and a man in the boat, smoking a pipe and smiling.

The sea makes waves. The man smokes and smiles. He points right, and his boat veers right. He points left, and his boat veers left—and this with no mast, nor oars, no rudder!

The sea gets upset, sends wave after wave, each bigger than the last. The man smokes and smiles, his boat rocking on the water.

The sea sends an iceberg, to which the boat sticks, and together they float—veering left when the man points left, and right when the man points right.

The sea froths and boils. There appears a giant walrus, its maw open wide, its teeth ready to tear the boat apart. But the man only smiles. He blows smoke from his pipe, and the walrus disappears.

The sea becomes wroth. There appears a great whale. It thrashes its tail, and the boat begins to sink.

The boat lies in the deep, but the man cannot be found.

He is not in the deep. He is not on the water. Only I lie asleep on the seashore.

The sea wakes with a sigh; and I wake with it, sighing also. My boat is no longer with me. It is floating freely on the wide-open sea—with a sail and oars and a good rudder. All that it lacks is me—its captain.

I become afraid. I run back and forth along the seashore, but the boat floats further and further away.

I speak to the sea.

Sea, you are large—and I, man, am small. You are strong, and I am weak. You are rich and I am poor. For what do you need my miserable boat? Do you not hold the *Kolyma* in ice all year round? Did you not block the path of the ice-breaker *Litke* on route to Wrangel Island, or the *Stavropol* on route to Nizhnekolymsky? Did you not wreck the schooner of that American, Svenson, swallowing all of its goods? Do you not send countless AKO freighters and steamers to your depths year after year?[1] For what do you want my miserable boat? Oh! Why must the strong be cruel, and the rich greedy? For what do you need my miserable boat?

And the sea thinks . . .

---

[1] Translator's note: Aktsionernoe Kamchatskoe Obshchestvo (Kamchatka Joint-Stock Company).

Yes, man, you speak the truth. I am large, while you are small. I am strong, while you are weak. I am rich, while you are poor. Indeed, for what do I need your miserable boat?

And the sea begins to roll—and lo! a miracle: my boat floats ashore. Oh! miracle of miracles: the great are good, the strong are not cruel, the rich are not greedy! My boat floats ashore and whispers, "*Yetti!*"[2] And all that has transpired is not a dream—it is real.

You laugh. You don't believe me. But I swear it is true, by the beak of a crow, by the head of a bear. Now come on to my hut, and I will show you.

---

[2] Translator's note: *Yetti*, a general Chukot greeting. Eroshenko translates it as "hello."

CHUKCHI ELEGY

I AM LYING on the seashore; my dog is sleeping next to me.

My boat is dozing on the sea. There's a blue sky above, colorful stones below, an unswimmable ocean in front, and an unwalkable tundra behind. I hear the murmur of a stream pressing itself to the breast of the great sea. The summer day stretches endlessly. The August sun warms the arctic earth, me, my dog, my boat . . .

Everything beneath this soft sky and on this warm earth is asleep. No, not everything. Listen! a gunshot! Another. Indeed, the rich don't sleep. From the water there comes the fearful cry of ducks; a flock of grebes takes flight; seagulls burst into tears. A crow shrieks.

Oh, Crow! Why do you wish evil on this shore?

The sea turns in its sleep. The tundra yearns in its dream.

Oh, rich man! When will you sleep also?

Mosquitoes buzz round me, alight on my hand, and suck my blood. They cannot live without blood, mosquitoes—like man: he too cannot live without blood.

Oh, Crow! You are such an evil bird!

I touch the stones and speak to them, saying, "Once you were boulders; someday you will be sand; and later on, you will be dust. We will all be dust—me, my dog, and my boat.

Oh, Crow! You are such an evil bird!

BIBLIOGRAPHY

FURTHER READING

Akita, Ujaku. *Akita Ujaku Nikki*. Vol. 1–2. Tokyo: Miraisha, 1965.

Alexander, Agnes Baldwin. *History of the Bahá'í Faith in Japan: 1914–1938*. Edited by Barbara R. Sims. Tokyo: Baha'i Publishing Trust of Japan, 1977.

Bowen-Struyk, Heather and Normal Field, eds. *For Dignity, Justice, and Revolution: An Anthology of Japanese Proletarian Literature*. Chicago: University of Chicago Press, 2016.

Farquhar, Mary Ann. *Children's Literature in China: From Lu Xun to Mao Zedong*. London: Routledge, 1999.

Fujii, Shōzō. *Eroshenko no toshi monogatari: 1920-nendai Tōkyō, Shanhai, Pekin*. Tokyo: Misuzu shobō, 1989.

Hirabayashi Taikō. "Eroshenko." In *Hirabayashi Taikō Zenshū*, 376–402. Tokyo: Ushio Shuppansha, 1979.

Hwang, Dongyoun. *Anarchism in Korea: Independence, Transnationalism, and the Question of National Development, 1919–1984*. Albany: State University of New York Press, 2016.

Jones, Andrew F. *Developmental Fairy Tales: Evolutionary Thinking and Modern Chinese Culture*. Cambridge, MA: Harvard University Press, 2011.

Keith, Elizabeth M. *Dōshinshugi and Realism: A Study of the Characteristics of the Poems, Stories, and Compositions in Akai Tori from 1918 to 1923*. PhD diss., University of Hawai'i, 2011.

Khar'kovskiĭ, A. S. *Mōmoku no shijin Eroshenko*. Translated by Yamamoto Naoto. Tokyo: Kōbunsha, 1983.

Konishi, Sho. *Anarchist Modernity: Cooperatism and Japanese-Russian Intellectual Relations in Modern Japan*. Cambridge, MA: Harvard University Press, 2013.

Leduc, Amanda. *Disfigured: On Fairy Tales, Disability, and Making Space*. Toronto, Canada: Coach House Books, 2020.

Mine, Yoshitaka. "Vivo kaj verkoj de Vasilyj Eroŝenko." In *La kruĉo da saĝeco*, edited by Mine Yoshitaka, 69–88. Toyonaka: Japana Esperanta Librokooperativo, 1995.

O'Keeffe, Brigid. *Esperanto and Languages of Internationalism in Revolutionary Russia*. London: Bloomsbury, 2021.

Osipenko, Nikolaj. "Esplor-agado pri Vasilyj Erosxenko en Asxhxabad (Turkmenio)." *Ligo internacia de blindaj esperantistoj*, October 30, 2018. http://www.libe.slikom.info/Erosxenko-Konkurso/Nikolaj%20Osipenko%20(Rusio).htm.

Shibayama, Junichi, ed. *Vivis, vojaĝis, verkis—Ikita, tabishita, kaita—Esearo omaĝe al Vasilyj Eroŝenko, 1890–1952—Eroshenko seitan 125-shūnen kinen bunshū*. Tokyo: Japana Esperanto-Instituto, 2015.

Shi Chengtai. "Eroŝenko en Ĉinio." In *Cikatro de amo*, edited by Mine Yoshitaka, 79–100. Translated by Shi Chengtai and Hu Guozhu. Toyonaka: Japana Esperanta Librokooperativo, 1996.

Sōma, Kokkō. *Mokui—Meiji, Taishō bungaku kaiso*. Tokyo: Hōseidaigaku shuppankyoku, 1982.

Sutton, Geoffrey. "Vasilyj Eroshenko." In *The Concise Encyclopedia of the Original Literature of Esperanto 1887–2007*, 107–113. New York: Mondial, 2008.

Takasugi, Ichirō. *Hitosuji no midori no komichi: Eroshenko wo tazuneru tabi*. Osaka: Riveroj, 1997.

——. "Eroshenko no shōgai." In *Eroshenko zenshu*, Vol. 3, 9–236. Tokyo: Misuzu shobō, 1959.

Tonkin, Humphry, ed. *Esperanto: Language, Literature, and Community*. Translated by Humphry Tonkin, Jane Edwards, and Karen Johnson-Weiner. Albany: State University of New York Press, 1993.

Utsu, Kyōko. "Washīri Eroshenko no dōwa to Sōma Kokko." *Bulletin of Seisen-jogakuin Junior College* 1 (1983): 13–23.

Wada, Kiichirō. "Eroshenko kun to ukuraina e." In *Wakaki Sovieto to koi no horō*, 207–226. Tokyo: Sekai no ugokisha, 1930.

Xu, Xiaoqun. *Cosmopolitanism, Nationalism, and Individualism in Modern China: The* Chenbao Fukan *and the New Culture Era, 1918–1928.* Lanham, MD: Lexington Books, 2014.

Zipes, Jack. *Fairy Tales and the Art of Subversion.* 2nd ed. New York: Routledge, 2006.

SELECTED BIBLIOGRAPHY OF VASILY EROSHENKO

Because of the complicated nature of Eroshenko's bibliography—that he wrote in many languages; that the source text for his works is not always clear; that he published versions of his stories in various formats; and, last, that his works are still being rediscovered—I have chosen to limit this biography to works pertinent to this collection.

COLLECTED WORKS (IN CHRONOLOGICAL ORDER)

Yoakemae no uta. Tokyo: Sōbunkaku, 1921.

Includes the following tales originally written or published in Japanese: "Semai kago" [A Narrow Cage], "Sakana no kanashimi" [The Sad Little Fish], "Gakusha no atama" [The Scholar's Head], "Numa no hotori" [By a Pond], "Washi no kokoro" [An Eagle's Heart], "Matsunoko" [Little Pine], "Haru no yoru no yume" [A Spring Night's Dream], "Kawari neko" [The Mad Cat], "Mushūkyōsha no junshi" [The Martyr], and "Kanariya no shi" [The Death of the Canary].

Saigō no tameiki. Tokyo: Sōbunkaku, 1921.

Includes the following tale originally written or published in Japanese: "Futatsu no chisana shi" [Two Little Deaths].

La Ĝemo de Unu Soleca Animo. Shanghai: Orienta Esperanto-Propaganda Instituto, 1923.

Includes the following essay, poem, and tale originally written or published in Esperanto: "Unu paĝeto en mia lerneja vivo" [Some Pages from My School Days], "Homarano" [Humanity], and "Rakontoj de velkinta folio" [Tales of a Withered Leaf].

Jinrui no tame ni. Tokyo: Tōkyō Kankōsha, 1924.

Includes the following tales originally written in Japanese: "Jinrui no tame ni" [For the Sake of Mankind] and "Chōchin no hanashi" [The Tale of the Paper Lantern].

Xìngfú de chuán. Translated by Lu Xun, Xia Mianzun, Ba Jin, Hu Yuzhi, Jue-nong, Xike, and Wei Huilin. Shanghai: Kāimíng shūdiàn chūbǎn, 1931. Includes the following tales translated into Chinese, of which the source text is lost: "Xiǎo jī de bēijù" [The Tragedy of the Chick], "Hóng de huā" [The Red Flower], and "Shíguāng lǎorén" [Father Time].

UNCOLLECTED WORKS (IN CHRONOLOGICAL ORDER)

"Fukkatsusai no hi" [Easter]. *Mitsuboshi no hikari*, 151–152 (June 28–July 28, 1916).

"Akai hata no moto ni—tsuihō ryokōki" [My Expulsion from Japan]. *Kaizo* (September 1923).

"La ĉukĉa elegio" [Chukchi Elegy]. *Esperanta Ligilo*, no. 3 (1933).

"Ĉukĉa idilio (Rakonto de ĉukĉo)" [Chukchi Pastoral]. *Esperanta Ligilo*, no. 4 (1933).

WEATHERHEAD BOOKS ON ASIA

LITERATURE

David Der-Wei Wang, Editor

Dung Kai-cheung, *Atlas: The Archaeology of an Imaginary City*, translated by Dung Kai-cheung, Anders Hansson, and Bonnie S. McDougall (2012)

O Chŏnghŭi, *River of Fire and Other Stories*, translated by Bruce and Ju-Chan Fulton (2012)

Endō Shūsaku, *Kiku's Prayer: A Novel*, translated by Van Gessel (2013)

Li Rui, *Trees Without Wind: A Novel*, translated by John Balcom (2013)

Abe Kōbō, *The Frontier Within: Essays by Abe Kōbō*, edited, translated, and with an introduction by Richard F. Calichman (2013)

Zhu Wen, *The Matchmaker, the Apprentice, and the Football Fan: More Stories of China*, translated by Julia Lovell (2013)

The Columbia Anthology of Modern Chinese Drama, Abridged Edition, edited by Xiaomei Chen (2013)

Natsume Sōseki, *Light and Dark*, translated by John Nathan (2013)

Seirai Yūichi, *Ground Zero, Nagasaki: Stories*, translated by Paul Warham (2015)

Hideo Furukawa, *Horses, Horses, in the End the Light Remains Pure: A Tale That Begins with Fukushima*, translated by Doug Slaymaker with Akiko Takenaka (2016)

Abe Kōbō, *Beasts Head for Home: A Novel*, translated by Richard F. Calichman (2017)

Yi Mun-yol, *Meeting with My Brother: A Novella*, translated by Heinz Insu Fenkl with Yoosup Chang (2017)

Ch'ae Manshik, *Sunset: A Ch'ae Manshik Reader*, edited and translated by Bruce and Ju-Chan Fulton (2017)

Tanizaki Jun'ichiro, *In Black and White: A Novel*, translated by Phyllis I. Lyons (2018)

Yi T'aejun, *Dust and Other Stories*, translated by Janet Poole (2018)

Tsering Döndrup, *The Handsome Monk and Other Stories*, translated by Christopher Peacock (2019)

Kimura Yūsuke, Sacred Cesium Ground *and* Isa's Deluge: *Two Novellas of Japan's 3/11 Disaster*, translated by Doug Slaymaker (2019)

Wang Anyi, *Fu Ping: A Novel*, translated by Howard Goldblatt (2019)

Paek Nam-nyong, *Friend: A Novel from North Korea*, translated by Immanuel Kim (2020)

Endō Shūsaku, *Sachiko: A Novel*, translated by Van Gessel (2020)

Jun'ichirō Tanizaki, *Longing and Other Stories*, translated by Anthony H. Chambers and Paul McCarthy (2022)

Dung Kai-cheung, *A Catalog of Such Stuff as Dreams Are Made On*, translated by Bonnie S. McDougall and Anders Hansson (2022)

Vasily Eroshenko, *The Narrow Cage and Other Modern Fairy Tales*, translated by Adam Kuplowsky (2023)

HISTORY, SOCIETY, AND CULTURE

Carol Gluck, Editor

Takeuchi Yoshimi, *What Is Modernity? Writings of Takeuchi Yoshimi*, edited and
translated, with an introduction, by Richard F. Calichman (2005)
Contemporary Japanese Thought, edited and translated by Richard F. Calichman (2005)
Overcoming Modernity, edited and translated by Richard F. Calichman (2008)
Natsume Sōseki, *Theory of Literature and Other Critical Writings*, edited and
translated by Michael Bourdaghs, Atsuko Ueda, and Joseph A. Murphy (2009)
Kojin Karatani, *History and Repetition*, edited by Seiji M. Lippit (2012)
The Birth of Chinese Feminism: Essential Texts in Transnational Theory, edited by
Lydia H. Liu, Rebecca E. Karl, and Dorothy Ko (2013)
Yoshiaki Yoshimi, *Grassroots Fascism: The War Experience of the Japanese People*,
translated by Ethan Mark (2015)